Praise for
.In Defiance

The historical significance of Quebec's colossal 2012 student strike is destined to be the subject of debate for years to come. With incisive clarity and intelligence, *In Defiance* shines in its analysis of the province's so-called Maple Spring. Co-spokesperson of Quebec's largest student union during the strike, Gabriel Nadeau-Dubois places the conflict within the context of a broad neoliberal attack on the Quebec model of socio-economic development, explaining how the movement faced down a barrage of insults, legal intimidation, contempt and violence from journalists, politicians, and the police and persevered to win substantial public support in the streets and at the polls. As ever, Nadeau-Dubois's voice elevates public discussion about the kind of world we want to live in and will be sure to resonate with readers the world over.

— Jarrett Rudy, Associate Professor of History, McGill University

In Defiance is a remarkable insider's account of the largest popular mobilization in recent Canadian history. With wit and clarity, Gabriel Nadeau-Dubois provides an engaging window into the 2012 Maple Spring and the role of the Quebec student movement as one of the leading forces challenging neoliberalism today.

— Yves Engler, author of *The Black Book of Canadian Foreign Policy*, former Vice President of the Concordia Student Union

In Defiance is as assertive as the demonstrations that overwhelmed Montreal's streets in 2012. It is a crucial book for Canadians. It gives insight into events that have shaped Quebec's political culture, such as the Quiet Revolution, which placed importance on education and called for free tuition. It exposes the breadth and depth of the student movement, which infused Quebec with ideas, reinvigorated our sense of street-level democratic participation, and demanded to know: how and by whom is our future to be shaped?

— Kaie Kellough, writer/poet, Montréal

In Defiance is a must-read for today's students and activists, and for anyone needing a renewal of faith in the future of humanity. Superbly written, with clarity and self-awareness, this book captures the idealism, practicalities, frustrations, failures, and victories of the Maple Spring. In addition to revealing the tactics, day-to-day challenges, and political realities happening behind the scenes of one of the largest student movements in recent history, Nadeau-Dubois shows us that – even against an entrenched government, bolstered in its suppression of the disenfranchised by a wider culture of social apathy – youth, intelligence, and hope can always rise and challenge those in power and, more importantly, the ways of thinking that keep them there.

— Mark Edelman Boren, author of *Student Resistance: A History of the Unruly Subject*

In Defiance

Gabriel Nadeau-Dubois

Translated by Lazer Lederhendler

Foreword by Naomi Klein

Between the Lines
Toronto

In Defiance

Originally published in French as *Tenir tête,*
© Lux Éditeur, Montréal, 2013
www.luxediteur.com

English translation
© 2015 Lazer Lederhendler

First published in English translation in 2015:
Between the Lines
401 Richmond St. W., Studio 277
Toronto, Ontario   M5V 3A8
1-800-718-7201
www.btlbooks.com

Library and Archives Canada Cataloguing in Publication

Nadeau-Dubois, Gabriel, 1990–
[Tenir tête. English]
    In defiance / by Gabriel Nadeau-Dubois ; translated by Lazer Lederhendler.

Includes index.
Translation of: Tenir tête.
Issued in print and electronic formats.
ISBN 978-1-77113-182-7 (pbk.). – ISBN 978-1-77113-183-4 (epub). –
ISBN 978-1-77113-184-1 (pdf).

    1. Student strikes – Québec (Province).   2. Student movements – Québec (Province).   3. Québec (Province) – Politics and government – 2003–2012. I. Title. II. Title: Tenir tête. English.
LA418.Q8N3313 2015   371.8'109714   C2015-900601-5
                                                                                                            C2015-900602-3

Cover design and photos by Jennifer Tiberio
Page preparation and text design by Steve Izma
Printed in Canada

RECYCLED
Paper made from
recycled material
FSC
www.fsc.org   FSC® C103567

We acknowledge the financial support of the Government of Canada through the National Translation Program for Book Publishing, an initiative of the *Roadmap for Canada's Official Languages 2013–2018: Education, Immigration, Communities,* for our translation activities. We gratefully acknowledge assistance for our publishing activities from the Canada Council for the Arts, the Ontario Arts Council, the Government of Ontario through the Ontario Book Publishers Tax Credit program and through the Ontario Book Initiative, and the Government of Canada through the Canada Book Fund.

Canada Council
for the Arts

Conseil des Arts
du Canada

Canadä

ONTARIO ARTS COUNCIL
CONSEIL DES ARTS DE L'ONTARIO
an Ontario government agency
un organisme du gouvernement de l'Ontario

To my mother and father, who passed on to me
their love of people and of justice.

The whole history of the progress of human liberty shows that all concessions yet made to her august claims have been born of earnest struggle. . . . If there is no struggle, there is no progress. Those who profess to favor freedom, and yet depreciate agitation, are men who want crops without plowing up the ground. They want rain without thunder and lightning. They want the ocean without the awful roar of its many waters.

— Frederick Douglass

Contents

Foreword

Naomi Klein

The Maple Spring in Quebec ushered in the biggest social mobilization this country has seen in decades. Its consequences will be felt for years to come in Quebec, but it will influence the rest of Canada only if those outside the province better understand what made it unique. This book, written by one of the country's most inspiring young leaders, does a great deal to help.

In early 2012, Quebec's students went on strike against massive hikes to university tuition fees. But instead of simply protesting the latest round of increases, the student movement told Quebec what they stood *for*: free, universal education, which they saw as a precondition for any just society. They also showed persuasively that the barriers being erected for poorer students were a reflection of a wider pro-corporate agenda, the reversal of which would be necessary if they were to achieve their goal.

By making a non-reformist, ambitious demand, their protests lit a spark in the province and opened up a broad debate about what kind of society Quebecers actually wanted. Outside the province, many of us watched as the movement unleashed an incredible wave of creativity and militancy. There were the witty videos, the gorgeous art, the poetry and music. There was the omnipresent red square – a must-have symbol of solidarity, which I eventually spotted even in the streets of Toronto. Most iconic, however, were the unforgettable images of hundreds of thousands of people, young and old, regularly crowding the downtown streets, many of them banging pots and pans on their balconies and in their neighbourhoods.

Through 2012, we watched as the students dreamed in public. We read in their manifesto how they envisioned the key features of Quebec life – not just education, but also health care, culture, energy, the land and rivers – protected and nurtured as a common inheritance, not gripped and disfigured by the logic of the marketplace. They exhorted us to think generations ahead, echoing the Indigenous worldview that long predates our country. It was this vision more than anything else that captivated Quebecers and so many of us beyond its borders. This was more than a mere "demand" – it was an expression of a rising cultural shift, an altering of the sense of what is possible.

These students were born around 1990, in the years when market fundamentalism reached its full ideological ascension; they have no memory of life before neoliberalism reigned supreme. All their lives they have heard that "history is over," that there is no alternative to unrestrained capitalism, that they should be satisfied with the perks of this atomized existence, happily distracted by their gadgets. But Quebec's students decided to flip their given script on its head. "We know now that history never ends," Gabriel Nadeau-Dubois writes. "There is always a springtime waiting in the wings."

Radical movements like theirs are invariably mocked and vilified by the political establishment, and for a very good reason: they can accomplish what that establishment fears most. They can make people believe change – broad, sweeping change – is possible. Most dangerous of all, they can win. In September 2012, after six months of political turmoil, the student movement helped oust Quebec's Liberal government. The newly elected Parti Québécois quickly repealed the tuition hikes, as well as a draconian law introduced by the Liberals to crack down on protest.

The English-language media's coverage of these events, however, left many Canadians poorly informed about what had actually transpired. This book is an excellent corrective, an eloquent tour of the heady months of 2012. Nadeau-Dubois recounts the astounding attacks the students endured – high-profile pundits comparing them to terrorists, legal intimidation, police violence. And he shares an insider's firsthand knowledge of the behind-the-scenes preparation that went into the making of the Maple Spring.

In an age when we need to rapidly recover the know-how of creating mass movements, the Quebec students have a lot to teach. At their height, such moments of widespread awakening and radicalization can feel like magic. Yet, as Nadeau-Dubois describes so vividly, they are hardly created with fairy dust – they are built by organizations, through tiring, often mundane work over many months or years. This story also shows that, despite the allure and power of social media activism, there is still nothing to compare to patient, face-to-face organizing. And it demonstrates that direct democracy – which many of the students practiced in general assemblies – can catalyze remarkable transformations, sweeping thousands who have never identified with activism into the life of a social movement.

When these tactics were combined with the students' bold vision of the far more equal world for which they were fighting, it proved unstoppable. At a time when so much needs fixing in our country, with unimaginably high stakes, these are lessons we would all do well to learn.

May 2015

Preface to the English Edition

Quebec at the Crossroads: The Roots of the 2012 Students' Spring

> Whoever does not link the question of education to the social
> question as a whole is condemned to fruitless dreams and efforts.
> — Jean Jaurès

The book you are about to read was drafted during the months that followed one of the largest citizens' campaigns in the history of Canada. It tells the inside story of a social conflict that, for more than six months, saw the Quebec student movement stand up to the provincial authorities in response to the government's decision to increase university tuition fees by 75 per cent. Readers are no doubt aware of the global context of this movement. In the majority of developed countries, the 2008 financial crisis had served as a pretext for the introduction of more radical neoliberal economic policies; everywhere, austerity measures gave rise to considerable social strife. The protesters of the Occupy movement in the United States and elsewhere, the *indignados* of Europe, the students of Quebec – each group in its own distinctive way refused to foot the bill for a crisis caused by the greed of the powerful.

Yet the mobilization of Quebec's youth took place against a particular background, one that warrants a fuller explanation. Quebec's cultural and political ecosystem is different in many ways from that of other parts of North America. This book, then, which details the events of the spring of 2012 in La Belle Province, should be situated within the wider environment. It is my hope that readers outside Quebec – those for whom the English translation is primarily intended – will benefit from this historical overview, for I am firmly convinced that this movement holds important lessons for social movements throughout the world.

The Actors

From February through August 2012, Quebec students waged a strike against the government of the Liberal Party of Quebec (PLQ), led by Premier Jean Charest, a veteran of Quebec and Canadian politics, who was in his ninth year as head of the provincial government. He had begun his political career in Ottawa in 1984 as a Member of Parliament for the Progressive Conservative Party of Canada and was soon appointed to the Cabinet by Prime Minister Brian Mulroney, becoming the youngest federal minister in Canadian history. Charest made a name for himself during the 1995 Quebec referendum campaign, where he played a prominent role in the camp opposed to independence. His accession to the leadership of the PLQ is believed by many observers to have coincided with that party's final break with the remnants of its social-democratic legacy. Indeed, he came to power in 2003 promising to carry out an ambitious "re-engineering of the state" and committed, in veiled terms, to abandoning Quebec's welfare state. His administration would be attended by confrontations with the labour movement and corruption scandals. When the student strike was in the offing in the winter of 2012, Charest was already under serious suspicion as to his personal role in those scandals. A few months earlier, he had been forced to retreat on the contentious issue of shale gas development in the St. Lawrence River valley. His power was on the wane, but everyone knew that this old warhorse of Quebec politics still had a few tricks up his sleeve.

On the opposite side, student resistance was being organized through three major provincial bodies. As spokesperson for one of them, the Coalition large de l'Association pour une solidarité syndicale étudiante (CLASSE, the broad-based coalition of the ASSÉ, the association for student union solidarity), I became known to the general public. As its name suggests, the CLASSE, which had been set up in December 2011 in preparation for the coming clash with the Liberal government, was a *temporary* coalition of student organizations assembled around a *permanent* body, the ASSÉ, founded in 2001. That year, a handful of Québécois cégep (junior college) and university student associations had decided to found an openly progressive, Quebec-wide student union that would draw on the democratic and action-oriented models of the alter-globalization movement and radical unionism. From the outset, the new student association demarcated itself from the two other province-wide student organizations, which the left regarded as too close to the Parti Québécois (PQ) and lacking in militancy. In 2005, a few years after Jean Charest's Liberals took power, the ASSÉ went all out and launched a general strike against a controversial reform of the province's system of student loans and bursaries. As a result of this successful struggle, the ASSÉ – despite some ups and downs – steadily grew in strength. In the fall of 2011, when it was becoming clear that an unlimited general strike was unavoidable if the Liberals' tuition hike was to be stopped, the ASSÉ decided to open its ranks to non-affiliated student associations and to those affiliated with other province-wide organizations, in order to establish a broader coalition for the duration of the impending struggle. The CLASSE was born. It soon numbered one hundred thousand, with members from more than sixty student associations throughout Quebec. Over the next few months, the CLASSE emerged as the main agent of mobilization, representing between 50 and 70 per cent of the striking students. The length and tenacity of the movement was in part the result of the CLASSE's role in the students' common front, whose other components were the Fédération étudiante universitaire du Québec (FEUQ, the Quebec university students' federation), with Martine Desjardins as president, and the Fédération étudiante collégiale du Québec (FECQ, the Quebec cégep students' federation), whose president was Léo Bureau-Blouin. The two federations represented the pragmatic, cooperationist tendency within the Quebec student movement; however, both of them joined the campaign and were at the centre of the negotiations with the Charest government.

The Setting

When the movement was just getting underway in February 2012, both camps were aware that what was explicitly at stake – the tuition fee increase – was rooted in a more fundamental clash of values. From the very beginning of the mobilization, the determination of the Liberal government was manifest. This resolve can be attributed in particular to the political circumstances surrounding the outbreak of the strike. The announcement of the tuition fee hike was part of a clever reframing of the Liberal plan to "re-engineer the state," now dubbed a "cultural revolution" by Finance Minister Raymond Bachand, the premier's right-hand man. The new label was hardly an exaggeration. The Liberal government's intentions were clear: to reorganize Quebec's public services according to the user-pay principle and to the detriment of the progressive tax policies typical of social democracy. The tuition hike was presented in the 2010–11 budget as a key element in an ambitious fiscal plan that involved the pricing and privatization of public services in Quebec.

The highly symbolic nature of the decision to raise tuition fees goes a long way to explaining why it triggered the "Quebec Spring." Low tuition fees are at the heart of what is referred to as the "Quebec model" of social solidarity. Still today, it is among the public policies that distinguish the political culture of Quebec from that of other North American jurisdictions. Furthermore, the student movement has long been one of Quebec's most powerful social movements; for over forty years, it was at the forefront of the struggle to make higher education more accessible, first to francophones and then to the children of working people. The spring 2012 mobilization was the tenth major student walkout since the 1960s. Most of those actions had resulted in complete or partial victories. By increasing tuition fees, Jean Charest's Liberals aimed to achieve a twofold objective: to demolish a strong political symbol, and to permanently cripple popular resistance to their neoliberal project.

In using the expression "cultural revolution," the Liberal minister displayed a remarkable degree of sincerity, because for Jean Charest and his cabinet, it was all about breaking with the political legacy of another revolution, the one known as Quebec's "Quiet Revolution." While this notion continues to nourish debates and reinterpretations among historians, it is most commonly defined as a brief but intense period of economic, social, political, and cultural upheaval in Quebec society in the 1960s and 1970s. The historian Denis Monière encapsulates it this way: "The era of clerical and political conservatism and of social and intellectual inertia gave way to an era of progress, social and cultural change and the revalorization of the political and of nationalism."[1] Thus, the Liberals' 1962 election victory under the leadership of Jean Lesage and the memorable slogan "masters in our own house" was followed by a raft of reforms affecting almost every area of Quebec society: education and health were secularized and nationalized, a network of public universities was created, public health insurance was introduced, a number of state-owned companies were established, hydroelectricity was nationalized, progress was made toward gender equality, the welfare state came into being, laws protecting the French language were passed, the pro-independence movement arose, and so on. Ironically, the first journalists to recognize how swiftly and radically Quebec was changing were from English Canada. In fact, the expression "Quiet Revolution" originally appeared in an article in Toronto's *Globe and Mail*. In sum, when Jean Charest and his ministers spoke of "re-engineering the state" or "cultural revolution," they basically sought to dissociate themselves from the social democratic legacy of that earlier revolution.

The attacks against the Quebec model of social solidarity were not a bolt from the blue. Jean Charest's coming to power in 2003, as already noted, represented an acceleration of the turn to the right that Quebec's political elites had initiated in the aftermath of the 1995 referendum. Following the traumatic defeat of the "Yes" side, Lucien Bouchard (a former Conservative Member of Parliament won over to the cause of independence a few years before), newly chosen to lead the Parti Québécois, made the rapid attainment of "zero deficit" his top priority when he became premier of Quebec in 1996. To that end, he carried out a series of colossal cutbacks in public services. His relentless accountant's approach provoked a groundswell of protest, particularly in the health sector. Nurses went so far as to launch an illegal strike to defend their employment standards. The PQ's swing to the right significantly damaged the party's longstanding ties with social movements, especially labour unions. All this added momentum to an already existing trend on the left: a growing number of progressives were organizing outside the party founded by René Lévesque. At the same time, the alter-globalization wave swept through the province, reaching its high point in 2001 with the mass demonstrations against the Summit of the Americas in Quebec City. It was in the wake of these events that the ASSÉ was created. A few years later, progressive elements disappointed with the PQ joined with labour activists and feminists in founding Québec solidaire (QS), which went on to become the first authentically left-wing party to win a seat in the National Assembly. The events of 2012 should be seen as the culmination of the headway made by Quebec's social movements over the previous fifteen years, in parallel with the rightward shift of the province's political elites, both Liberal and Péquiste (PQist). The widespread exasperation that people expressed by banging on pots and pans can be ascribed at least in part to the conformist managerial mentality that has stymied Quebec politics since the 1995 referendum defeat.

This was the multifaceted backdrop against which the drama of the 2012 spring played out. The main protagonists were, on one hand, a government determined to accomplish the neoliberal revolution conceived ten years earlier, and on the other, a student movement in peak condition, nourished by the democratic practices of the alter-globalization movement and radical unionism. When the strike began, both sides were aware that Quebec was at a crossroads.

The Events

The campaign officially began on February 12, 2012, once the threshold set by the CLASSE – twenty thousand students with a strike mandate – had been crossed. Initially, the mobilization was confined to a few university departments in Montreal and Quebec City, but very quickly it snowballed beyond any of the Coalition's forecasts. After only two weeks, the strikers' ranks had increased more than sixfold: 132,000 cégep and university students had walked out. On March 22, the campaign reached its first peak, with over three hundred thousand students on strike and about an equal number of people marching in the streets of Montreal; later that same day, the government issued a statement saying that it was "not impressed." Over the ensuing month, owing to the Liberals' stubborn refusal to negotiate with the student organizations, tensions continued to mount on the campuses of Quebec. Opponents to the strike swamped the provincial courts with requests for injunctions; dozens were granted, forcing classes to resume, but the vast majority of them could not be enforced. Meanwhile, more and more citizens were joining the weekly protests, and the CLASSE came out in favour of turning the campaign into a broad-based citizens' movement. The struggle was dragging on dangerously, but the strike mandates did not falter. The government hardened its discourse, relying on the media's negative coverage of the movement and striving to marginalize it vis-à-vis public opinion. The situation had reached an impasse.

On May 4, during the Liberal Party's convention in Drummondville, the accumulated tension exploded when a demonstration called by a coalition of community and union groups degenerated into a skirmish with the Sûreté du Québec, the provincial police. Twelve people were hurt, two of them seriously. A young Montreal student was blinded in one eye. For a few hours, a troubling report spread through the movement of a young cégep student who had died from his injuries. Fortunately, this proved to be untrue. While the fighting raged, I, together with other student representatives, was in the middle of a negotiation marathon with Liberal ministers in Quebec City. The next morning, with the tragic events in Drummondville making headlines, the minister of education and the three student organizations announced they had reached an agreement in principle. Over the following days, the students, revolted by the police violence and the Liberals' meagre offer, overwhelmingly rejected the proposed agreement at their general assemblies. One consequence of this rejection was quite unexpected. Ten days on, Line Beauchamp, the minister of education and vice-premier of Quebec, resigned all her positions and announced that she would be withdrawing from active politics for good. The news sent shock waves through Quebec's political scene and dealt a heavy blow to Jean Charest's government. The woman the premier chose to replace Beauchamp was one of his long-time associates, Michelle Courchesne; she immediately summoned the student associations to a fresh round of negotiations. At the same time, rumours began to circulate of a special law being drafted by the government in order to end the walkout. On May 17, three days after the new minister's appointment, Jean Charest tabled Bill 78, which was passed the very next day under the title *An Act to enable students to receive instruction from the postsecondary institutions they attend.* The law was composed of three parts. First, it turned the students' strike into a lockout by suspending the sessions of any establishments on strike at the time of its adoption and by imposing a timetable for the resumption of classes in mid-August so as to "restore calm" on the campuses. Second, the law forced administrators and faculty to dispense courses and strictly forbade anyone from directly or indirectly hindering normal campus life. Third, it obliged organizers of any gathering of more than fifty people to inform the police, at least eight hours in advance, of the event's date, time, duration, and location or route, in the case of a march. The law moreover gave the police the extraordinary prerogative to modify that route. The last two sections of the law also provided for exceedingly hefty fines. The heavy-handed piece of legislation left most political commentators aghast, including those favourable to the government's position on tuition fees. While the bill was being debated in the National Assembly, popular support for the student movement was being expressed in concrete ways. Starting on May 19, tens of thousands of citizens marched in the streets each night, banging on pots and pans to protest the malicious law. The noisy demonstrations soon took on huge proportions. In the end, the only effect of Jean Charest's strong-arm tactics was to energize the mobilization even further.

On May 21, shortly after the enactment of Bill 78, the CLASSE concluded its weekly convention by publicly stating that it would disobey the law and by inviting the population to join in a demonstration of civil disobedience to be held the next day at noon. The response was overwhelming. On May 22, the one-hundredth day of the strike, more than 250,000 people marched in solidarity with the students, in open defiance of the special law. Four days later, five hundred lawyers wearing their courtroom gowns paraded through downtown Montreal to show their indignation at the passing of this repressive law. Also that day, negotiations resumed between the new education minister and the student movement – to no avail. After three days of deliberation, the minister declared that she was abandoning efforts to reach an agreement with the strikers. Behind the scenes, we understood what this meant: the province would be going to the polls.

Our intuition would be confirmed on August 1, when Jean Charest called an early general election for September 4. The news threw the movement off balance, and, one after the other, student associations voted to go back to school. The night of the elections, the verdict came down. Jean Charest and his government were defeated. Pauline Marois was chosen to lead a Parti Québécois minority government. There was no mistaking the import of her first act: she officially cancelled the tuition fee increase and abrogated the special law. At the same time, she declared that a summit on higher education (Sommet sur l'éducation supérieure) would be held, in her words, to consult those directly concerned on the best policy to adopt with regard to tuition fees.

Since 2012

At the time of writing, more than two years have elapsed since the end of the students' campaign. Today, its overall assessment and the lessons to be drawn are still under discussion. The re-election of a majority Liberal government in the spring of 2014 has led many to express serious doubts about a mobilization that had been regarded as "historic" and to wonder whether it had all been in vain.

I myself am naturally inclined to be prudently optimistic. I understand the disappointment felt by a number of activists. Some of them believed, often justifiably, that the campaign of 2012 could have been the catalyst for qualitative social changes. My studies in sociology over the past few years have helped me to put such expectations in perspective; societies are complex organisms whose evolution is necessarily slow.

Yet, with regard to the accessibility of higher education, the students' campaign won a clear victory. The Liberals' goal, it should be recalled, was to raise university tuitions by 75 per cent and to index them to the cost of living indefinitely. The Quebec-wide consultation organized by the Parti Québécois during its brief tenure led to the indexation of tuition fees to families' disposable income. Of course, this is not a step toward free education. But to deny that this is a gain would be to judge the movement very harshly indeed. There is, after all, a huge difference between a spectacular increase and conditional indexation. Over the coming years, tens of thousands of young Québécois will be able to enter university. This is no small matter. The mobilization of 2012 will have succeeded in safeguarding Quebec's unique approach toward access to education. Today, higher education remains more accessible in Quebec than anywhere else in North America.

The Liberals' return to power was disconcerting for many people, including me. Despite a painful defeat in September 2012, the current Liberal government has shown an astonishing level of determination in relaunching the neoliberal revolution that the student movement had originally halted. As expected, the Liberals' official position on university funding is to support indexation. A great deal of political courage would have been required to take on the student movement once again. But on a host of other issues, the austerity offensive of Philippe Couillard's government represents a more radical, accelerated version of the political changes initiated under the leadership of Jean Charest: increased childcare fees, a major overhaul of the health system, the reduction of public health prevention measures, assaults on pension plans, cutbacks in the civil service.

As I write these words, it is difficult to foresee whether or not the response of ordinary Quebecers will be as radical as the Liberals' austerity plans. One thing, however, is clear: this time, there can be no question of the student movement marching in the streets alone. Faced with the brutality of the austerity measures, the people of Quebec are turning to the labour movement, without which it will be impossible to prevail. At union meetings, there is already talk of following the example of the students who mobilized in 2012 and, like them, of standing in defiance.

Montreal, November 2014

Acknowledgements

Thanks, first, to my former colleagues of the CLASSE executive: Jean-Michel Thériault, Élise Carrier-Martin, Philippe Éthier, Guillaume Legault, Philippe Lapointe, Maxime Larue, and Guillaume Vézina. One of the reasons for the success of this great, beautiful strike was undoubtedly its solid and experienced Quebec-wide team, including, in particular, the executive. This has not been noted often enough, especially within the student movement. Thank you, dear friends. Thank you for the camaraderie and for your patience. Thank you for your confidence, which at times I did not deserve. Thank you for supporting and defending me in the dark hours, for putting me in my place when I had it coming, and for being demanding when that was called for. I will forget the long meetings, and I will forget our shouting matches, but I will never forget the pride I felt at being among you during this first great battle of our generation. Thank you, Jeanne, for having shared with me a difficult and thankless job.

Thanks to Renaud, my "spin," my friend, my brother. I would never have survived this dream without you. Thanks to Cloé, for being there, for listening, for understanding in my moments of doubt, anger, sadness, and exhaustion. Thanks to Gabrielle, Anne-Marie, Ludvic, Keena, Julien, Benoît, and Joëlle, my partners in mischief, my comrades-in-arms and in revelry. Thanks to Arnaud, my loyal friend for so long, who reminds me, when necessary, of the importance of being present for people, for the ones I love. Thanks to Rico, my friend and mentor, lover of Quebec and its inhabitants, for his vitality, his guidance, and his appreciation. Thanks to Simon, for the advice that often got me out of a tight spot. Thanks to Christian, for the hope. Thanks to Évelyn, Étienne, and Gabrielle, who responded so generously to my public appeal for financial support. Thanks to Marie-Claude, Frédéric, Léda, Jean-Philippe, and Jean-Sébastien, for those endless nights at the Bistro brainstorming the title for this book.

Thanks to Keena and Julia for their research assistance. Thanks to Alexandre for the proofreading. Thanks, in particular, to Mark, my guide on this first, perilous, and liberating publishing adventure, for finding the words when I faltered.

Finally, for this English edition, I wish to express my gratitude to Jessie Hale for her editorial work and to everyone at Between the Lines. Thanks to Lazer Lederhendler, who not only beautifully translated this book, but above all captured the spirit and the essence of my words.

Chronology

February 2012[1]

7 February The first strike vote is held at the Collège de Valleyfield. The results are close: 460 for, 448 against, 1 abstention.

13 February The threshold of twenty thousand students from seven associations and at least three different campuses is reached. The strike begins.

14 February Eleven thousand students at the Université du Québec à Montréal and Université Laval launch an unlimited general strike.

16 February Lise Payette refers to the "Québécois spring" in her column in *Le Devoir.*

20 February 132,000 students are on strike. The Mouvement des étudiants socialement responsables du Québec (Movement of socially responsible students of Quebec), opposed to the strike, makes its appearance in the media. Their symbol is the green square, in contrast to the red square worn by the strikers.

March

1 March The minister of education, Line Beauchamp, states: "The decision has been made."

1 **March** Between three thousand and eight thousand students rallying in front of the legislature in Quebec City are driven away by police using tear gas.

5 **March** 125,000 students are on strike.

15 **March** Between four thousand and five thousand people join the annual demonstration against police brutality in Montreal. The police arrest 226 individuals.

18 **March** A family-oriented demonstration in support of the strike, organized by the CLASSE, brings together thirty thousand people in Montreal.

22 **March** A milestone in the strike: 305,000 students out of a total of 400,000 are on strike. More than 300,000 people rally in Montreal. The mood is festive.

22 **March** The Commission scolaire de Montréal (Montreal School Commission) comes out in support of the students.

27 **March** According to Radio-Canada, about five hundred people, including students and locked-out Rio Tinto Alcan workers, march in Alma.

April

3 **April** A student, Laurent Proulx, is granted an injunction so that he can attend his anthropology course at Université Laval.

4 **April** Nearly two hundred thousand students are on strike.

6 **April** The Université du Québec à Chicoutimi obtains a temporary injunction forbidding students from demonstrating less than twenty-five metres away from the establishment.

11 **April** Premier Jean Charest denounces the "intimidation" practiced by the students. He compares the climate in the student general assemblies to that prevailing in the construction industry.

12 **April** Students at the Collège de Valleyfield shut down courses despite the administration's opposition to the strike vote. In an open letter to the newspapers, more than five hundred university professors express their support for the striking students.

13 April Jean-François Morasse, a visual arts student at the Université Laval, is granted an injunction so that he can attend his courses.

14 April A family-oriented rally whose theme is "For a Québécois Spring" assembles forty thousand people in Montreal.

22 April In Montreal, between 150,000 and 300,000 people rally for Earth Day.

23 April An estimated 185,000 students are on strike.

24 April Line Beauchamp demands a truce during the upcoming negotiations. The first of some one hundred nighttime marches is held.

May

3 May Pauline Marois, head of the Parti Québécois, announces that if elected premier, she will limit the tuition increase to the cost of living index.

4 May The government summons the unions, students, rectors, professors' associations, and the Fédération des cégeps to a round of negotiations.

4 May Two thousand people rally for a protest march in Victoriaville during the Quebec Liberal Party convention. The event soon turns into a clash with the SQ (the Quebec provincial police), and twelve individuals are injured, two of them seriously: Alexandre Allard suffers a severe head injury, and Maxence L. Valade loses the use of an eye.

5 May After twenty-two hours of negotiations, an agreement in principle is signed. The tuition increase is not affected, but its consequences are attenuated through administrative measures. The agreement is later massively rejected by the student associations.

14 May Line Beauchamp announces her resignation. Michèle Courchesne steps in as minister of education. The new minister summons the students to a meeting.

14 May The chief justice of the Superior Court, François Rolland, declares that the non-respect of the injunctions "saps the credibility of the legal system."

15 May The SQ's riot squad intervenes at the Collège Lionel-Groulx to oust demonstrators protesting against the injunction by blocking the doors of the institution. Yves Marchotte, communications director of the college, states: "We have just proven, for all Quebec to see, that an injunction is not the right way to ensure that students return to classes."

15 May Gabriel Nadeau-Dubois is accused of contempt of court.

17 May Jean Charest tables Bill 78, titled *An Act to enable students to receive instruction from the postsecondary institutions they attend.* The bill provides that the academic term will be suspended in cégeps and universities affected by the strike, demonstrators will be heavily fined, and the right to demonstrate will be restricted.

18 May Over ten thousand individuals take part in the twenty-fifth nighttime demonstration, largely in protest of the special law.

19 May In response to the special law, citizens go into the streets every night at eight o'clock to participate in pots-and-pans demonstrations.

21 May The CLASSE announces that it intends to disobey the special law.

22 May A major demonstration marking the one hundredth day of the strike sees between 200,000 and 250,000 people marching in the streets of Montreal, according to Radio-Canada.

25 May The pots-and-pans movement spreads throughout Quebec.

28 May In Montreal, five hundred lawyers wearing their courtroom gowns rally in the downtown area to denounce the special law. On May 29, the minister of transportation, Pierre Moreau, calls for the organizer of this protest, François Desroches-Lapointe, a jurist for the SAAQ (Quebec automobile insurance corporation), to be sanctioned by the state.

28 May Negotiations with the government are resumed.

31 May The negotiations break off.

June

8 **June** Laurent Proulx drops the anthropology course for which he had obtained an injunction.

22 **June** Large "twenty-second-day-of-the-month" demonstrations are held. In Quebec City, there are between three thousand and five thousand marchers, while tens of thousands rally in Montreal.

July

13 **July** The CLASSE publishes its manifesto, *Nous sommes avenir* ("We are the future" or "We are what is to come"), and tours Quebec to explain its positions to the population.

20 **July** The mayor of Trois-Pistoles threatens to withdraw grants from the Échofête (a yearly music and environmentalist event) if Gabriel Nadeau-Dubois takes part.

August

1 **August** Jean Charest calls a general election for September 4.

8 **August** The students at the Collège de Valleyfield decide to end their strike.

9 **August** Gabriel Nadeau-Dubois announces that he is stepping down as CLASSE spokesperson.

19 **August** A debate is held among the leaders of the major parties as part of the election campaign. The debaters accomplish the remarkable feat of barely mentioning the most serious political crisis that Quebec has known in forty years.

September

4 **September** A minority PQ government is elected. Charest is defeated in his riding.

October

27 October Pauline Marois and Pierre Duchesne call into question the underfunding of universities.

November

3 November Gabriel Nadeau-Dubois is found guilty of being in contempt of court.

3 November The CLASSE is dissolved.

Introduction

Better to go farther with someone than nowhere with everyone.
— Pierre Bourgault

Every story has a beginning, and for me the adventure of the spring of 2012 began on June 12, 2009, when I read the front page of the Montreal daily *Le Devoir*. One of the headlines caught my attention: "Towards a new tuition fee hike."[1] The article reported that the Université du Québec à Montréal (UQAM)[2] had presented a plan to achieve a balanced budget calling for an annual tuition increase of one hundred dollars as of the fall of 2012. The university's rector, Claude Corbo, was reported to have said that his estimates were based on those of the provincial government. Yet the fee increases that had been applied since the fall of 2007 were supposed to end after five years. Something was amiss. The next day, the office of the minister of education, Michelle Courchesne, denied everything. But the damage had already been done; the student movement was taken aback.

At the time, I was on the committee in charge of putting out *L'Ultimatum*, published by the ASSÉ, L'Association pour une solidarité syndicale étudiante (Association for student union solidarity), a student union that, despite its forty thousand members spread over more than thirty associations, was relatively unknown. The banner headline of the first issue of the 2009 school year read, "Tuition hikes in 2012? Fees unfrozen once more." And so began the long, hard work of researching, informing, mobilizing, and stepping up pressure tactics, all of which would culminate in the confrontation of the spring of 2012. But in 2009 we had no idea that we were cooking up one of the biggest political conflicts that Quebec had ever known. The cauldrons of history are unpredictable.

In March 2010 the budget was tabled and the tuition increase was confirmed. Two days before the official announcement, the Liberal finance minister, Raymond Bachand, addressing a group of business people, declared that the budget would amount to a veritable "cultural revolution." The minister must have been aware of the allusion to a dark moment in the history of Communist China, when thousands of intellectuals and academics were humiliated and massacred. We wondered, somewhat aghast, what message the minister of finance was sending the students by referring to the imminent tuition hikes in such harsh terms. Yet the radical shift that his speech heralded was not a bolt from the blue. During the previous months, the Charest government had mandated a committee of experts[3] to establish a diagnosis of the state of the province's economy and public finances. From the lofty heights of their authority as economists, the committee members, to no one's great surprise, pronounced the Québécois economic model moribund. Their report essentially rehearsed the conclusions spelled out five years earlier in Lucien Bouchard's "Manifeste pour un Québec lucide (Manifesto for a clear-sighted Quebec)" – in the wake of the student strike of the spring of 2005 – to the effect that Quebecers were living beyond our means. Quebec's "economic backwardness," the immeasurable burden of its public debt, fierce international competition, and the dogmatic requirement to maintain a balanced budget, all made it impossible to collectively finance public services. The clear-sighted ones, or "*lucides*," as they came to be known, saw just one choice: adopt their program or go bankrupt amid unspeakable suffering.

Such were the underpinnings of Raymond Bachand's March 2010 defence of his revolutionary budget, which included increases in electricity rates and daycare fees as well as a "health tax." We can no longer afford the status quo, he repeated at every opportunity. The universities were at the heart of the outdated model that needed to be deconstructed; the budget provided for a considerable but unspecified rise in tuition fees as of the fall of 2012. The government declared that in the coming year it would meet its "partners" in the academic world to discuss the details.

Premier Jean Charest's troops must have bitterly regretted that hasty announcement. They overconfidently gave the student movement two years to prepare for battle. The official confirmation of the tuition hikes did nothing but spur the students' mobilization, at least as far as the ASSÉ was concerned.

A few weeks after the Bachand budget was submitted to the National Assembly (the Quebec provincial legislature), I was elected to the executive of the student union as communications secretary. At the time, activism did not have the sheen of glamour that it would acquire at the height of the strike. Handing out flyers, doing the rounds of classes, and raising awareness – our efforts were generally met with widespread apathy, if not outright contempt. On December 6, in the middle of a winter storm, the ASSÉ nevertheless succeeded in mobilizing several thousand people in Quebec City just when the academic "partners" were meeting to determine the extent of the fee increases. Knowing that the purpose of this exercise was merely to apply a veneer of political legitimacy to a *fait accompli*, and true to its position in favour of free education, the ASSÉ convention decided to boycott the event. On the day of the demonstration, the two other student organizations, the Fédération étudiante universitaire du Québec (FEUQ, the Quebec federation of university students) and the Fédération étudiante collégiale du Québec (FECQ, the Quebec federation of cégep[4] students), arrived at the same conclusion and walked out of the meeting. The student mobilization on the streets of the provincial capital exceeded our expectations. We returned to Montreal, our toes frozen stiff and our hearts full of hope.

In the spring of 2011, Bachand played out the last act of the Liberal comedy and announced a fee increase of $1,625 spread over five years. The response was swift. In late March the pressure tactics were ratcheted up. A number of campuses affiliated with the ASSÉ voted for a daylong walkout, and thousands of angry students paraded through the streets of Montreal. At the same time, a few key offices were occupied. At that point I was already a spokesperson, and I was struck by the widespread public indifference toward our demands. Whenever possible, I hammered home the message that in the absence of a response from the Liberal government, we would consider launching an unlimited general strike. Radio silence. We were ignored.

We pursued our preparations throughout the summer: training activists, holding conferences, producing campaign material. Following a major gathering of Quebec student organizations, the call went out for a unitary march in Montreal on November 10, 2011. The debates within the national[5] organizations were numerous and strained. To everyone's surprise, the turnout for the demonstration was beyond all expectations. Despite the rain and the cold, nearly thirty thousand students streamed through the streets of the city. Across Quebec, student assemblies voted for strike days. The spokespersons repeated via the media that the students truly wished to be consulted on the issue of the fee hikes. As spokesperson for the ASSÉ, acting on a resolution adopted by the Association, I asked the government to meet with the student organizations in order to avoid a strike.

The November 10 demonstration was our last chance to be heard by the government. Yet in spite of the students' show of force, the government's only response was silence. On that day, together with tens of thousands of other students, I realized that we would have to go on strike. All the other pressure tactics had failed, and the coming spring term would be our last chance to stop the increase. We either went on strike against it or we passively accepted it, along with everything it entailed. No other option was open to us. On December 4, the ASSÉ opened its ranks to all the student associations in Quebec, whatever their affiliation. Many of them were to join us for the duration of the conflict. The Coalition large de l'ASSÉ, the CLASSE (Broad-based coalition of the ASSÉ), was born. It would play a vital role in the strike.

Officially, what was at issue in the coming confrontation was the tuition fee increase, but both camps realized that the stakes of the conflict involved far more fundamental values. The Liberals were aware of the radical nature of their reform; they knew that if they defeated the students, a formidable foe would be out of their way. For forty years, the Quebec student movement had been an ardent champion of the social project that the Liberals intended to undo. A victory over the students would send a powerful message to other social movements, especially the trade unions, as to the government's determination to push ahead with its neoliberal agenda. Conversely, if the students prevailed, their success would curb – at least for a time – the right-wing "cultural revolution." Both camps undertook the great struggle of the spring of 2012 fully cognizant of what they had to lose.

o o o

I wrote this book in order to reflect on what the strike brought to light about us, the people of Quebec, and to consider how it changed our lives, mine in particular. What follows is the story of neither the student movement nor the CLASSE. Within the coalition that I publicly represented, I was part of a tendency that other activists criticized for being pragmatic and for caring about public image. This affects my account of the strike, which is not the official story, but my own. It is the story of a person who spent most of the strike in meetings of the CLASSE's decision-making bodies or in media forums – one vantage point among many. But from where I stood during the spring of 2012, the view was unique, to say the least. And I felt it was one worth sharing.

A host of stories about the student strike of 2012 could be written – and I hope they will be – by activists with very different experiences of that extraordinary campaign. It was a manifold movement, and we must be wary of those who in the coming years will want to lay exclusive claim to its meaning. No one holds a monopoly on the truth of that moment, but there is nothing to keep us from trying to understand it. Out of the dialogue among the various interpretations of the strike, its historical meaning will eventually emerge, and this book is no more than my contribution to that crucial exploration. My essay looks back to what was, but my true interest lies in what will be. I am too young for commemorations, and the strike is not yet a museum piece. I am deeply convinced that the social crisis of 2012 has not had its final say; by revisiting its key moments, by "descending into the real," to quote the historian Jean-Marie Fecteau, we will find sustenance for the necessary political actions that await us.

With this in mind, we must go beyond the sensational images repeated ad nauseam on TV. In one of his best-known speeches, Pierre Bourgault[6] said, "Respectability is not about image. It is something you achieve when, after some years, you find that you have stayed true to your original objectives, true to your original principles and your original dreams. You see, what is not respectable today may be so tomorrow; this is as true for men and women as it is for ideas." For many people in Quebec, the student strike was not respectable. It bothered them and destabilized their strongly held beliefs. At times I actually had the impression that this was the main grievance against us: above all, whatever the outcome, the turmoil had to stop. The students did not succumb to the panic. They did not give in to the injunctions of those pretending to be reasonable. They were beaten but did not cave in. They were confident enough not to accept the vilification of their hopes. They refused to believe that hushing up problems and running away from conflict could resolve anything. They may be the ones to have restored the dignity of political debate. Certainly, it was the students who rediscovered a custom that had been lost in Quebec: defiance.

Part 1

Three General Assemblies

{ One }

A Twelve-Vote Margin

Nothing is too difficult for youth.
— Socrates

"Here, today, at the Valleyfield Cégep, History is watching you. History is watching you and offering you a choice: whether or not to make your mark. What you do today will be remembered. The decision you make will tell future generations who we were. And you already know what is being said today about our generation. That we are the generation of comfort and indifference, the generation of cash and iPods; that we are individualists, egotists; that we don't care about anything, except our navels and our gadgets. Aren't you tired of hearing this? Well, I am. Luckily, today we have a chance to prove that it's not true, that it has never been true.

"I'm going to stop here, but before I do I want to tell you a secret. I don't want to go on strike. I'm afraid of going on strike. I may appear confident standing here, but, you know, this is my first strike, too. I wasn't there in 2005. My fears are the same as yours. I have no idea what to expect in the weeks to come.

"But I'm going on strike anyway. I don't want to go on strike, but I'll do it, because I know that together we are strong. Because even though when I'm alone, I'm afraid, I know that, together, we can do this. I'm going on strike, Quebec is going on strike, and I hope you will join us. Because I want us, together, to stop the tuition hike."

o o o

That is how I ended my speech at the general meeting of the Association étudiante du Collège de Valleyfield (Collège de Valleyfield student association) on February 7, 2012. It surely was not the best speech, or the most exciting. But none of the few other speeches I've made in my life have seemed as important or as difficult to deliver.

That Tuesday, the students at the Collège de Valleyfield were gathered in their school auditorium to decide whether or not to declare an unlimited general strike. They were the first cégep students to have to make that decision. I knew, we all knew, that the first strike vote at the cégep level would be the most important, the most decisive. The very next day, students at the Marie-Victorin Cégep would have to choose in their turn, to be followed by those at Mont-Laurier, Matane, Vieux-Montréal, and so on for weeks to come. If Valleyfield voted against the strike, the consequences for the movement were likely to be disastrous. It would send a signal of demobilization that would probably prompt the other associations to stay in class. We were afraid of a domino effect. Fully conscious of what was at stake, I felt strained to the point of paralysis.

We were all haunted by the failure of 2007, when the students were facing a 30 per cent increase in tuition fees. The universities had voted in favour of striking, but the cégeps refused en masse to join the walkout movement. The first cégep to hold a vote was Vieux-Montréal, a historical bastion of the student movement. The students there decided to stay in class, dealing a fatal blow to a strike movement already struggling to take off. Over the following days and weeks, the motions in favour of striking were rejected, one after the other. The strike was never able to get off the ground. The exact reasons for this failure may be hard to ascertain, but its consequences are unmistakable. Between 2007 and 2012, tuition fees rose 30 per cent amid widespread indifference;[1] on the strength of that apathy, the Liberals felt free to announce a further 75 per cent increase for the 2012–17 period.

We had learned from experience how strategically important the cégeps were. They are governed by a law requiring mandatory eighty-two-day teaching sessions. Theoretically, every strike day must be made up for, such that it is virtually impossible to cancel a session. For how can you get tens of thousands of students to retake their courses when cégeps on Montreal Island are already operating at maximum capacity, and with a new crop of high school graduates arriving each fall? The large number of cégep students is not the only significant factor; the modus operandi of these institutions exerts economic, bureaucratic, and legal pressure on politicians. Without the cégeps, a strike would not be doable. We knew this. A poor showing in Valleyfield might stymie the mobilization in the other cégeps – we knew that too. We simply could not afford to lose this vote.

The local cégep activists were highly motivated and their arguments were tight, but they lacked experience. The last walkout at Valleyfield had taken place in 2005, so none of the members of the student association had ever organized a general meeting to decide on a strike, which is why the timetable set by the CLASSE's national coordination team had placed Valleyfield in the second wave of cégeps scheduled to go on strike. This cégep was supposed to follow the movement, not launch it. The plan had been upset at the previous general assembly, when several dozen students opposed to the strike had forced the executive to hold a vote two weeks before the appointed date. They were well aware that the sooner the vote was held, the better their chances of seeing their position prevail, because the mobilization call-out would be less publicized and, more importantly, the strike movement would not yet have gained any momentum.

Valleyfield therefore became a province-wide priority for the CLASSE. Each day, students from the four corners of Quebec came to help the local activists impress upon the student body the importance of the upcoming plebiscite. All day long, mobilization teams covered the cégep's hallways and rooms, distributing thousands of newspapers and flyers. No method was deemed too unorthodox to pique the students' interest; members of the local association even set up a "strike couch" in front of their office. The idea was simple: any student could stretch out on it and express her or his fears regarding the strike. Activists from the association executive and the mobilization committee took turns, so that someone was always available to listen to students who needed to talk.

For the two weeks preceding the Valleyfield ballot, mobilization trumped sleep. I don't recall ever witnessing another campaign as intense and harrowing as this one. It is a crucial point that bears repetition: losing in Valleyfield was not an option.

When I showed up there, a few hours before the vote, the tension in the association office was at the breaking point. The campus was, to use the activists' jargon, "saturated." After two weeks of constant effort, it was practically impossible to find a student who was unaware of the imminent assembly. At dawn, we were still fine-tuning the organizational details of the event. Nothing could be left to chance. In the middle of the room, surrounded by local militants, my colleague Maxime was doing his best to facilitate the huddle. Some distractedly broke off in midsentence. Others kept nodding off. They were exhausted. They had spent the whole night planning the assembly minute by minute. The resolutions had been divided up among the team members, and the various arguments to be used had been set down on index cards; everyone knew exactly what to say and when. Scattered around the student association office, forgetting the fatigue and the strain, the activists rehearsed what they had to say and corrected each other. One of them would deal with tax issues; another would refer to the victories of the Quebec student movement over the years; still another would focus on the question of access to higher learning.

As for me, I had been asked to speak at the beginning of the meeting. On arriving at the cégep, I had already worked out the key points of my speech, but as soon as I entered the office I realized it would have to be rewritten. Maxime, a Valleyfield graduate who had been there in 2005, would have liked to contribute to the meeting, but after two weeks of intense mobilization at the school he had already convinced everyone who was liable to be convinced by him, and he knew it. Still, he did have a very specific idea of what needed to be said. With the pressure on, we redrafted my entire speech. "You have to speak from the heart. Be honest," he told me. "People want to feel that you're one of them. Don't hide the fact that the strike can go in unforeseen directions. Just emphasize that it can empower us to change things. Tell them it's your first strike."

We headed over to the auditorium, which was steadily filling up. Close to a thousand students crowded into the hall, which was meant to hold eight hundred; they occupied every available space, including the stage. The members of the executive, clustered around Maxime, were furiously reviewing their notes. The chairperson installed himself at the front of the stage. Everything was ready. The meeting could begin. After a few questions of procedure were dealt with, one of the members of the executive submitted a motion in favour of the strike, and I took the floor.

"First, I think it's important to remember why we're here today, why we're obliged to talk about a strike. We're here because we're faced with one of the worst threats to the accessibility of higher education in the history of Quebec. We're faced with a 75 per cent rise in university tuition fees. There is nothing trivial or negligible about this. Don't forget that this comes on top of the increase already imposed by the Liberal government in 2007. In other words, if we accept this additional hike, tuition fees will have doubled since this government came to power.

"So the question is this: Why do they want to increase our tuition fees? We're told it's because the universities are underfunded. We're told that it's inevitable, that they must have more funding, and the only place where funds can be found is in our pockets. Isn't that odd, because as far as I can see there's lots of money in Quebec. It seems to me there's lots of money even in the universities. Enough, anyway, to be wasted on bad management, on advertising, on new buildings, and on lavish spending by university rectors. And the government, too, seems to have a lot of money. Enough, at least, for gifts to friends of the party and for handouts to the mining companies that will be profiting from Plan Nord;[2] enough money to lower the taxes paid by large corporations and by the wealthy. Funny, isn't it: apparently money is in short supply only when it's convenient for it to be in short supply.

"There is no lack of money in Quebec. And, no, there is nothing inevitable about the tuition fee hike. The hike is not an unavoidable consequence of accounting principles; it is a political scheme, a scheme being carried out at our expense. What are we going to do about it?"

o o o

I was so keyed up that today I can barely remember that moment. The only reason I can reproduce the speech here is because I kept a copy, a twisted piece of paper, misshapen by my nervous hands. But I do have a very distinct memory of the heated debate that followed.

The discussion period was emotional and acrimonious. Knowing that the vote would be close, the executive had submitted a cautiously worded resolution. If it was adopted, the walkout would not apply to any internships, so as not to unduly penalize students in special programs where they would be obliged to redo uncompleted internships the next year. However, to take advantage of the possibility of opting out, students from various technical programs stepped up to the mic one after the other to propose amendments designed to exempt their programs from the strike mandate. Nearly two hours of the meeting were spent voting on these amendments. Each time, someone from the executive took the floor to point out that a strike is a collective action whose meaning and impact depend precisely on its unifying effect. The executive constantly stressed that the teachers in charge of each study program had been consulted to ensure that the strike would not adversely affect the students' academic career in the long run. The procedures slowed down the meeting, and people began to grumble impatiently. Several voices called for the vote. Ironically, the loudest complaints came from the very students whose requests to be exempted from the strike mandate were causing the delays. Finally, after more than three hours of deliberation, the time came to vote.

Mindful of the extremely tense atmosphere in the hall and of the potential for intimidation from opponents to the strike, a member of the association's executive board came to the mic to ask for a secret ballot. The motion was seconded and put to the assembly. One of the leaders of the camp opposed to the strike then took the floor and asked the chair if the secret ballot would take longer than a show of hands. The chair answered that the executive board had made all the necessary preparations, but that it would obviously take more time for the assembled students to vote one at a time and then for their votes to be tallied. The student at the mic then spoke against the motion because he wanted to get it over with as quickly as possible. "I'm fed up and I want to go home!" he blurted out, setting off a wave of applause and shouts of approval. After that, to the executive's surprise, the motion to hold a secret ballot was defeated. The vote would be taken with a show of hands.

The chairperson officially put the strike resolution to a vote: "Those in favour of the motion, please raise your voting cards at this time." Several hundred small orange cards started to jiggle in the air. It was hard to say if they represented a majority. The chair took a long look and continued: "Those opposed to the motion, please raise your voting cards at this time." Other orange cards sprang up, once again in large numbers. A murmur ran through the hall; there was no way of knowing which side had carried the vote. No clear majority was apparent at a glance. The chair therefore invited two students who were for the strike and two who were against to join him at the front of the auditorium; he then asked them to count the number of votes on both sides one by one. The voting process was repeated: "Those in favour of the motion, please raise your voting cards at this time." Followed by the count. Again the chair addressed the assembly: "Those opposed to the motion, please raise your voting cards at this time." Followed by the count. Then the chair addressed the assembled students: "The four students have each in turn submitted very similar figures that point to the same results. In favour of the motion: 460 votes. Opposed to the motion: 448 votes. One abstention. The motion is carried."

A deafening clamour broke out. Instinctively, Maxime and I turned to face each other. "We're on strike!" he shouted with his hands in the air and tears welling up in his eyes. I clambered over the rows of seats that stood between us and jumped into his arms. "We're on strike! We're on strike!" he repeated. Twelve votes. We had won by a margin of twelve votes. So close, it was hardly possible. I was beside myself, ecstatic, like so many others around me. All over the auditorium people were hugging each other. Some shouted for joy, jumping up and down, crying; others were completely stunned and withdrew behind a wall of silence or quickly left the room.

But the meeting was not yet officially over. After the initial shock, the students opposed to the strike quietly regained their composure. The chairperson tried to restore some order. Little by little, some returned to their seats, while others stomped out of the auditorium. Amid the commotion, a student went to the mic to ask for a revote . . . with a secret ballot. The crowd froze. The assembly was plunged into a heavy silence. Had we been too quick to celebrate? The chairperson was visibly at a loss. He was loath to formally accept the proposal, but how could he not? In theory, it was possible to adopt a proposal for an immediate revote, but under the circumstances it would be problematic, to say the least. The vote had been taken a few moments earlier, but in the meantime several dozen individuals had left the room. Nevertheless, the question was put to the assembly for debate. A few opponents of the strike took the floor to demand a revote on the grounds that the vote had been too close to be valid. Supporters of the strike replied that the results of a revote would be skewed because the number of students in attendance had been drastically reduced. Confusion reigned. No one could predict the outcome of a revote. At this point a young man who was against the walkout – the one who had pressed for a rejection of the secret ballot – took the floor. He spoke almost directly to the section of the auditorium where most of the opponents of the strike were seated: "Listen, guys, we defeated the proposal for a secret ballot, and now we've lost. We have to accept the results. It's only a one-week strike mandate. We just have to come back the following week and win." I sensed a wave of discomfort sweeping over half the room; there was a growing realization that the outcome of the vote would have to be accepted.

Emerging from his haze, the chairperson spoke up. "Given that several dozen people left the room after the initial vote, I've come to the conclusion that a revote would constitute an infringement of the assembly's previous decision. Therefore, we will allow either an appeal of that decision or a motion to end the meeting, nothing else." In a last-ditch effort to annul the strike vote, a few students presented a motion challenging the chair's ruling, but this was quickly quashed. Finally, nearly four hours after it had begun, the meeting was brought to a close. Valleyfield was on strike. We had won the day.

The atmosphere in the auditorium was peaceful as it emptied out. The confusion and procedural wrangling that had gone on after the strike motion was passed had somewhat dampened our enthusiasm, but the meaning of what had just taken place slowly sank in. The first cégep – and not the least of them – had just voted in favour of the strike. Two years of preparing and mobilizing, and here we were. Not that it had been easy: twelve votes less and the campaign would have foundered.

The following day, eighteen hundred students at the Cégep Marie-Victorin adopted a mandate for an unlimited general strike, with 78 per cent in favour. The next vote was held by the student association of the cégep in Mont-Laurier, where the motion in support of the strike was carried with a solid 58 per cent majority. The strike was revving up.

Even now, I can't imagine what would have transpired had we lost the first vote at the Collège de Valleyfield. I don't know if the movement could have been set in motion. But one thing is clear: the events would have unfolded very differently. For most Quebecers, this major strike erupted out of nowhere. What the story of that first vote shows is how fragile and tenuous the source of that eruption actually was, how low-key compared with the sensational images of hundreds of thousands of young people marching in the streets during those spectacular rallies that would be televised throughout the spring of 2012. In the beginning, there was nothing spontaneous about the strike, despite what some enthusiastic observers eagerly reported. It was, on the contrary, the fruit of a long and often taxing mobilization effort accomplished by a handful of activists. Many of these students had to tune out the disparagement of their immediate social circles, going from one campus to the next, visiting cégep after cégep, not only to remind their peers of the importance of fighting for accessible education but also to defend the integrity and independence of our higher learning institutions against the profit-oriented plans of the Parti Libéral du Québec (PLQ), the Liberal Party of Quebec. To cite just one example, the car of one member of the Quebec-wide mobilization committee clocked up sixty thousand kilometres – one and a half times the circumference of the planet – in the span of a few months. These are the people who, at each assembly, made the difference between the strike and passive acceptance of increased tuition fees.

The launch of the strike opened up a fabulous space of creativity. There was a burst of artistic and militant initiatives full of colour and originality, which gave the impression that a spontaneous uprising of Quebec youth was taking place. Intellectuals, bloggers, and artists joyfully welcomed this unhoped-for – and so all the more surprising – upsurge of anger and political imagination. Too often, the far more humdrum and repetitive mobilization work that made it all possible – the sort of militant action disdained by many – was overlooked. No matter what the thrill-seekers may say, the strike was not a work of art, a merely expressive event. We were all moved by the beauty, inventiveness, and spontaneity of the spring of 2012, but none of it would have been possible without the stubborn efforts of activists who stayed out of the public eye. We may marvel at this phenomenal political moment, but if we ignore the energies that were deployed to bring it about, our praise will be meaningless, and, more importantly, we will run the risk of never again experiencing such events.

I will not deny, however, that at a certain juncture in that long springtime, there indeed was a tipping point, a qualitative leap that lifted us into an unpredictable and unique political space. This vast strike movement encompassed a complex range of multifaceted and shifting elements, but without the young women and men who were there from the start, none of it would have come about. Their hard work must be recognized and hailed as the indispensable – though admittedly insufficient in and of itself – condition that made it possible to open an extraordinary breach in the historical process. In Valleyfield, a mere twelve votes tipped the scales in our favour. But how many leaflets, how many hours of exertion paved the way for that frail margin? One can only guess. What is indisputable is that without organization, there simply would have been no vote.

As activists and, more broadly, as citizens, we cannot and will never be able to control either the political conjuncture or the collective forces at work in our society. But what we can do is to work tirelessly to keep democracy and political involvement alive by constantly fostering debate on our campuses, in our workplaces, and in our neighbourhoods. That is what happened in the spring of 2012. When Charest and his government threw down the gauntlet by drastically increasing tuition fees while refusing to engage in serious discussion with those directly affected, we were ready to take them on.

{ Two }

A Generation No One Was Counting On

M id-February. The campaign was in its infancy. The scene was Collège de Maisonneuve, one of the larger cégeps on Montreal Island, a stone's throw from the Olympic Stadium. The general assembly where the launch of the strike would be decided was about to begin. The movement had grown since Valleyfield. From one assembly to the next, the level of mobilization became more and more impressive. My habitual wariness was cracking; everywhere I went I saw thousands of students vote in favour of walking out. What surprised me most was how heterogeneous the movement was – strike votes were mushrooming, often without the CLASSE's foreknowledge. The *carrés rouges*,[1] red squares of cloth, were everywhere. This symbol of solidarity and resistance to higher fees for public services had first been introduced in October 2004 by an anti-poverty collective, and was then adopted by students during their strike of 2005. Now, once again, it adorned the coats of students of all ages and social backgrounds. A mood of cautious optimism was gaining ground among coalition activists. The mobilization was progressing apace, though we were aware that victory was far from assured. I still had moments of doubt as to the possibility of staying on strike until March 22, the date set for a major show of force by people from all across Quebec.

The students arrived en masse and streamed into a vast gymnasium. Fifteen minutes before the assembly was scheduled to begin, the hall was filled to capacity. The doors to a second, adjoining gymnasium were opened, and soon it too was teeming with young people. Finally, after some coaxing, everyone had found a place inside. Both halls were jam-packed with thirty-five hundred students in attendance, an all-time record according to the student association's archives. Never had so many students been seen in a general meeting at the Collège de Maison-neuve. Inside, the students were pressed together and already engaged in discussion. Some huddled in groups, deliberating and fine-tuning their arguments. The atmosphere was electric.

The chair declared the meeting open and gave the usual procedural explanations, but he was interrupted by the head of security, who approached and whispered something in his ear. When the chairperson spoke up again, instead of completing his presentation on procedures, he announced that the security services had asked him to convey an important message: at the end of the meeting, it would be advisable for the students to leave not all at the same time and not all in the same direction. Also, during the meeting students should refrain from jumping or making any other sudden, large-scale movements, because this might put undue stress on the building's structural integrity. The cégep's walls had not been designed to stand up to a gathering of this size! Immedi-ately, the whole crowd burst out laughing. Just imagine! The student mobilization was so massive that it threatened the very structure of the institution.

Following this unusual announcement, a member of the executive tabled the motion in favour of the strike. The debate began. From the very start, the tone was far more civilized than what I had witnessed in Valleyfield. This cégep had been affiliated with the ASSÉ for some time, and over the years a sense of decorum for general assemblies had taken root. People who came to the mic spoke more calmly. Those opposed to the strike knew there was nothing to be gained by flouting the rules; to carry the vote, they would simply have to win over a majority of those present.

The members of the student association executive were duly pre-pared. Each of them took the floor in turn to present a different aspect of her or his position. Step by step, they built a reasoned yet passionate case in favour of the walkout, deconstructing as best they could the prevailing myths about the strike as pressure tactic and about its consequences. It was up to the executive, essentially, to ease student anxieties by fielding the volley of questions on public finances, democracy, equal opportunity, and social justice. Other students spoke out against the strike, affirmed their right to attend classes, or defended the tuition fee hike. After an hour or so of discussion, the chairperson announced that the question would soon be put to a vote.

A few individuals were still waiting at the mic. Sitting alongside the members of the executive and the mobilization committee, I felt the tension go up a notch. We were all aware that those speaking last would have a crucial impact on the assembly. Their words would weigh heavily on the students' minds and might easily determine the outcome of the vote. Standing toward the end of the line was a young black man dressed head to foot in classic hip-hop style: low-slung trousers, baseball cap, gold chain around his neck – the works. He would be among the last to speak. At first glance, he hardly looked like your average activist, and he did not sport the red square that would identify him as pro-strike. Instinctively – our thinking is cunningly tainted by prejudice – I was afraid of what he might say. But I was mistaken. When his turn came, he began by upbraiding the previous speaker, who had vigorously opposed the strike: "You! You're against the strike, and I'm guessing it's because you can afford to go to university? Or maybe it's your parents who can afford to send you there? Am I right? Well, my friend, I want to go to university, and if there's a tuition hike I won't be able to. So what am I supposed to do? I ask you: What do I do?" He turned to address the room. "All those who are going to vote against the strike, raise your hands. Come on, raise your hands!" Little by little, students timidly raised their hands. Immediately he continued: "Okay, well, we want to go to university! We want to go, but we won't have enough money if they raise the tuition. Those who have enough money, are you going to help us pay for our college education? Are your parents also going to pay for us? No? Yes or no? No?" No one answered. "Well, then that just confirms what I thought." He went on: "If you don't want to pay for our education, I think we have to go on strike. That's right! Because it pisses me off that people can't go to university just because they don't have enough money. Yes, it pisses me off. So if there's one person in Quebec who is just five dollars short of his university tuition, well, for that person and for just five dollars, me, right now, I'm going to vote for the strike." The hall erupted with applause and shouting. The activists around me were exultant. Who would have thought the meeting would end on a note like that, coming from someone they had never once seen in the student association's office?

The young man's tirade, whose style and musicality are hard to render, was cheered not for its subtlety but because it was straightforward and genuine and therefore deeply moving. It was probably more effective than all the carefully crafted speeches of the student association activists. His words expressed the anxiety of hundreds of thousands of young Quebecers who saw their future being shut down by the threat of a $1,625 yearly rise in tuition fees. Starting with the simple fact of not having the means to attend university at that price, he asked those opposed to the strike a simple question: Would they be willing to pay for his university education? If so, there would obviously be no point in resorting to the strike. The lack of response from the hall – which the speaker had expected – was sufficient grounds for him to vote in favour of the strike. The whole debate on the redistribution of wealth was encapsulated in the young man's speech. According to his scenario, the fact that the richest citizens did not share their wealth effectively kept him from entering university. His message was clear: if wealth was not pooled in order to ensure universal access to education, then we had to go on strike – even for a single individual, even for a small sum of money. What's more, he shed light on the fundamental injustice of the user-pay principle, the new cornerstone of the state's economic and social policies. Levying the same fees on all those wanting to attend university did not amount to making everyone pay his or her "fair share," because the cost may be the same, but not incomes; the effect of higher tuition fees is not the same for all families. "You who have enough money, are you going to help us pay for our education?" Based on the user-pay rationale, the answer must be an unequivocal "No."

The general assembly of the College de Maisonneuve responded to this unfairness, so cogently brought to light, with an unlimited general strike mandate adopted by an 85 per cent majority.

○ ○ ○

A cégep literally shaken to its foundations by the mobilization of its students, an entire assembly taken aback by a young man's forceful speech, a vote unequivocally in favour of the strike. On that cold February day I realized that the close results of the Valleyfield meeting had not been representative of the strike now looming on the horizon. This observation may seem superficial or anecdotal, but it in fact attests to the exceptionally unifying nature of the spring 2012 student strike. Though the movement's first steps were faltering, the Maisonneuve assembly made clear that something altogether original was in the making. That night I sensed that the campaign of 2012 would be radically different from all those that had preceded it.

Over the following days, my intuition was confirmed. The first cégep walkouts had the anticipated effect. One after the other, cégeps and university departments voted in favour of strike mandates, often far more quickly than the CLASSE's province-wide coordination team had hoped. On March 1, barely three weeks after the strike was launched, the symbolic mark of 100,000 strikers was attained. A week later the number of strikers had reached 125,000. The pace of recruitment was unmatched.

The movement was expanding at a speed that even the most optimistic among us had not imagined. It was unprecedented. The mobilization advanced beyond the historical boundaries of the student movement. More than ever before, the walkout spread to the regions: Gaspé, Saint-Félicien, Rouyn-Noranda, Matane, Gatineau, Sherbrooke, Rimouski, Drummondville, Mont-Laurier, Quebec City. The strike covered the entire province, including, tellingly, certain departments of the main "Anglo" universities, Concordia and McGill, representing their first significant participation in a student strike. Elsewhere, departments traditionally resistant to mobilization now added their voices to the chorus of protest. Too rarely has it been mentioned that the medical students at the Université de Montréal went on strike for two weeks. At the same university, their colleagues in computer science and operations research also walked out. At the Université Laval in Quebec City, the physics students stayed away from their classes for over five months. The mobilization reached an initial high point on March 22, when, on the occasion of the mammoth national demonstration held by all three student organizations, a record 303,000 students were on strike. The list of associations on strike was long and wide-ranging, from the social sciences to biochemistry, not to mention the students at the École Polytechnique. This constituted the largest strike of any kind in the history of Quebec.

Even considering the amount of energy invested, the extraordinary work accomplished by the student association activists, and the high stakes involved, I am still amazed by the magnitude of this uprising. Many have said it before: no one expected young people to mobilize to this extent. I had been told so often that I belonged to an apolitical generation that I had come to believe it. And there was another die-hard prejudice that the strike held up to scrutiny. During the first weeks of the student mobilization, our critics described it as the action of a university elite defending its privileges and refusing to make the sacrifices necessary for the health of our public finances. We were spoiled babies, born with silver spoons in our mouths. Given their perception of "today's youth," this was the only way they could make sense of what was going on. For them, we were nothing but egotists incapable of giving anything back to society. But rather than railing against our selfishness, the naysayers would have done better to take a good look in the mirror. The accusation was not only groundless – as the transformation of the student strike into a general citizen's movement would soon show – but it actually betrayed the individualism of those who had levelled it. Their indictment of the student movement reflected their own view of the world, their own conception of politics as a tool to defend private interests, which they projected on us out of ignorance, resentment, or simply the inability to see reality in a new light. What they ultimately found intolerable in our discourse was that we were challenging precisely the generalized egotism that drives their politics. In the spring of 2012, the power elite tarred us with the brush of its own turpitude, and we proved them wrong.

○ ○ ○

I am part of the first post–Berlin Wall generation. I was born in 1990, a few months after the wall fell. I grew up in a world encompassed more than ever by a single political and economic system. The end of the Cold War sounded the death knell for freedom-hating political regimes, but it also created the illusion that there was no alternative to economic globalization, to the subordination of democratic sovereignty to the faceless laws of capital. Similarly, in Quebec – as far back as I can recall political events – only neoliberal governments came to power, and every one of them of course proceeded to privatize public institutions. The Parti Québécois (PQ) of my generation is the party of Lucien Bouchard, not that of René Lévesque.[2]

In a world where everything seems to be decided in advance, my generation was to inaugurate the "end of history." As it happens, this end turns out to be just the beginning of another history. More and more people today find themselves in a blind alley; in particular, young people in many countries are paying heavily for the foolishness of the neoliberal political economy. It was in this environment of global political ferment that the Quebec student movement arose. In Europe and Latin America, and even among our neighbours to the south, a growing portion of the population rejects the direction the elites are forcing the world to take. Everywhere, the watchwords echo each other; everywhere, citizens are busy opening up possibilities, reactivating the people's political imagination after three decades of Thatcher-style, management-oriented conformism.

That is certainly part of the answer to a question I've so often been asked since the strike ended: Why did the strike take on so much importance? Some of the reasons no doubt have to do with circumstances specific to Quebec. The unlimited general strike was aimed at a government weakened by corruption scandals and disliked by a large part of the population. This political environment unquestionably helped stimulate the student mobilization in the spring of 2012. But there was more. The social and political exhaustion of the conservative project of the last four decades was, in my view, a deep-seated factor behind the incredible strength of the spring 2012 protest movement.

Contrary to the eager assertions of Liberal ministers and certain columnists – I still have trouble telling them apart at times – the struggle against the tuition hikes was never used as a pretext to fight for a hidden "extremist" political agenda. From the very start, the activists of the student movement were fully cognizant of the political nature of their campaign. They never denied it. When they took the floor to speak in Valleyfield and de Maisonneuve at the beginning of the campaign, students were already referring to the redistribution of wealth, democracy, and fiscal policy. The central issue was education. The fact is, however, that one cannot raise the question of education without initiating the larger debate on the ultimate aims of all our collective institutions, because education is at the core of a society's social and cultural objectives. We were perfectly aware that a debate on access to university education opened onto a larger political and cultural confrontation. The Liberals would have liked to pass off their own objectives as merely administrative measures. But they, too, well understood that their decisions were means toward achieving ambitious and, in their own way, radical objectives. Wasn't their stubborn refusal to engage in dialogue a demonstration of ideological dogmatism? Their awakening in 2012, and that of many others, was such a rude one because they were convinced that no social force stood in the way of their conservative policies. Hubris – that was their fatal flaw. Perhaps they truly believed that history had indeed come to an end.

We know now that history never ends. There is always a springtime waiting in the wings.

{ Three }

The Hatred of Democracy

October 2011. I climbed up on the stage of the packed theatre at the Collège Lionel-Groulx. Ignoring the timetable set by the CLASSE's province-wide coordination team, the executive of the local student association had decided to ask for a mandate to launch an unlimited general strike two weeks ahead of schedule. The mass demonstration of November 10 was still weeks away – that's how much of a rush these students were in. The executive had invited me to come and start the debate by explaining the details of the tuition fee hike, as well as the pressure tactics that the ASSÉ had set in motion since March 2010. The general mood was tense; people were on edge. I had hardly begun to speak when voices shouted, "Shut the fuck up!" and "Let's vote, dammit!" Half the room broke out in laughter and applause, while the other half demanded an end to the uproar. Somewhat shaken, I went on with my speech, only to be interrupted once again. Abandoning my notes for a moment, I said, "If you didn't want to hear me out, then you shouldn't have adopted the motion asking me to speak. Now that it's been adopted, please let me finish out of respect for the assembly." I continued, trying to ignore the rising chorus of muttering and heckling. In spite of the shouts and boos of some and the irritated sighs of others, I went on with my speech, though I ended it in a hurry and not without stumbling over a phrase here and there.

I felt exasperated as I returned to my seat. The chair addressed the

29

assembly, reminding the students that without some degree of decorum the meeting would be drawn out unduly. Once the proposal to go on strike was tabled, the debate got underway. Immediately, the hostilities broke out anew, with waves of personal attacks and gutter-level language. The chair took the floor: "This meeting is a democratic space. I'm asking you to be polite. The debate, even when it heats up, can be healthy if we show mutual respect." Democracy? Mutual respect? Debate? A young man stepped up to the microphone and offered his personal interpretation of such notions: "Hey, here's what I think. The fucking hippies from visual arts that want to strike – well, why the hell don't they do it alone, eh?! Personally, I couldn't give a shit about their faggoty art projects. What I want is to finish my courses and get a job. Is that fucking clear? I've got no problem if they want to have their little marches, so long as they fucking leave us alone and let us study, dammit! And, oh yeah, by the way, this is taking much too long, so can we get on with the vote and go home?!" Once again, half the room broke out in laughter and applause, while the others, reduced to silence, sank into their seats. Given this atmosphere, the members of the executive, despite having carefully prepared their arguments in support of the strike, hesitated to take the floor. Some of them nevertheless ventured out, and soon paid the price. They were greeted with endearments – "Faggot!" "Fucking communist!" "Bum!" – that elicited cheers and laughter. A group of young men at the back of the hall added insult to injury with their ape-like shrieks: "Hoo-hoo! Hoo-hoo! Hoo!" When the chairperson attempted to restore some order, he was hooted down in his turn. The vote was taken amid the commotion and mayhem. Unsurprisingly, the gorillas won; the motion in favour of the strike was defeated by a very wide margin. I left in a daze. I had never witnessed a meeting as disgraceful as this.

Fortunately, the vast majority of general assemblies held in the spring of 2012 did not look like zoos. They proceeded in accordance with the basic rules of courtesy and respect that democratic discussion requires. Of course, the debates were often tense, strident, and sometimes exhausting, but those who took part in them were rarely in danger of sacrificing their dignity. Overall, the participants, including those opposed to the strike, behaved decently. The meeting at Lionel-Groulx was an exception. The point of describing it is to debunk the persistent notion that CLASSE activists manipulated the general assemblies and had no scruples about intimidating their opponents. A strike vote foisted on unwilling students would have had no legitimacy whatsoever. In fact, that assumption was an out-and-out lie. Those who, like me, witnessed the meetings will attest that the few confrontations that did occur were consistently instigated by students fiercely opposed to the strike. They were the ones who hurled homophobic, racist, or sexist insults or uttered personal threats. The columnist Richard Martineau was right to lament that young people should be "booed, shouted down, intimidated, and harassed when they dared to step up to the mic at general assemblies,"[1] but had he for once known what he was talking about, he would have been careful to point out that intimidation was the method preferred by the most fervent opponents to the strike.

It would be a grave injustice against the activists who built this movement if history were to record that they imposed the strike through the use of force or threats. A great deal of bad faith is needed to accuse them of being vandals who stifled dissent, as the Liberals and many commentators have insinuated. The student associations devoted themselves unreservedly to organizing and facilitating the democratic spaces that the assemblies represented. Those young, passionate activists did everything they could to ensure a healthy, inclusive climate that enabled everyone to speak freely. It would never have occurred to them to put their personal convictions ahead of democracy and challenge a vote against the strike. They ought not to be confused with the individuals who took legal action to invalidate collective decisions that went against their personal interests.

Certainly, the rules of order governing student meetings can be and sometimes have been used as tools by those wishing to control and muzzle debate, and I do not claim that this could never have happened during the spring of 2012. Some supporters of the strike raised their voices in general meetings and expressed their anger and impatience, but such outbursts were rarely meant to intimidate or silence their adversaries. By and large, the militants who initiated the strike movement and were involved in it from start to finish wanted more than anything to foster constructive, fruitful political debate. As avid advocates of direct democracy, they took pride in this. Furthermore, most of those who passed judgment on the general assemblies never attended a single one and were unaware that political discussion was constantly – some would say naively – encouraged. There were times when the commitment to democratic discussion proved cumbersome and disheartening, and tested the patience of many participants, but it also generated some incredibly fertile political exchanges.

The strike was one of the largest sites of civic education ever created in Quebec. For an entire year, in hundreds of general meetings, tens of thousands of people debated the future of an institution and its place in society. Inevitably, the decorum that such deliberation requires became second nature to the students, and over time disgraceful excesses like those witnessed at Lionel-Groulx grew quite rare. In fact, toward the end of the conflict, defenders of the tuition fee hike were seen on illegal picket lines when some administrations tried to forcefully impose a return to class. "Yes to the hike and yes to democracy" was the slogan on a placard adorned with green squares[2] that a young demonstrator waved while blocking the doors to the Cégep Saint-Jean-sur-Richelieu.

The Liberals and other detractors of the student movement also cast doubt on the strike's legitimacy by constantly complaining about what they described as the very low level of participation in the general assemblies, proving, in their view, that student democracy was only a facade behind which a small minority connived to foist its views on the majority (a reprimand – if the Charbonneau Commission findings are to be believed[3] – better suited to the friends of the Liberal regime than to the young strikers). The question of participation levels was a pretext for those demanding that student associations abandon their customary decision-making body, the general assembly, in favour of what they considered the fairer, more democratic method of the referendum or electronic voting, supposedly to put an end to intimidation. This proposition does not stand up to scrutiny.

Upon examination, there was little difference in the various pre-strike consultations between the results in general assemblies and those obtained through referenda or e-votes. In the Outaouais, the regional cégep launched the strike following a referendum with a 78 per cent participation rate and 65 per cent of votes in favour of striking. Similarly, after a referendum held on March 3, the student association in St.-Jérôme launched the strike with a participation rate of over 75 per cent and a 61 per cent majority in support of the action. In St.-Jean-sur-Richelieu, the referendum that set the strike in motion had an 81 per cent participation rate. Many would be very pleased if our provincial and federal elections elicited the same degree of enthusiasm. Meanwhile, cégeps like those in Mont-Laurier and Matane launched the strike through general assemblies with levels of participation in excess of 66 per cent and outcomes similar to those just cited. In St.-Félicien, the level of participation in the assembly was 75 per cent, with 56 per cent voting in favour of the strike. The case of the Cégep de Joliette is noteworthy because the students there voted on February 27 in a general assembly with a 65 per cent participation rate, and the mandate was later renewed until May 11 by e-vote. The electronic voting on April 13 at the Cégep André-Laurendeau in Montreal, organized with the aim of ending the walkout, had an 83 per cent participation rate and actually confirmed the decision of the general assembly to pursue the strike. The cégep administration had no choice but to abide by the results of the process that it had itself initiated and to recognize the strike until August 9.

To all appearances, the Liberals and the cégep administrations were not defending the virtues of democracy when they tried to dispossess the students of the sovereignty of their assemblies. The opponents of the strike never took seriously the pedagogical aspect of the general assemblies, any more than they did their highly democratic nature. As of mid-April, the college and university administrations endeavoured to break the strike movement by refusing to attribute even the slightest legitimacy to the students' collective decisions, on the pretext that the session had to be completed according to schedule. Held up to widespread scorn, disregarded by those in power, and subjected to police brutality – this was how the students were deprived, in a remarkably coordinated way, of their primary means of collective expression. The scorn reached its peak a little over a month later with the adoption of a special law[4] whereby the Liberals and the CAQists[5] muzzled student democracy, trampled on the freedom of expression, and institutionalized their own contempt. Students could well go on making democratic decisions, but their voices would no longer be heard, their political autonomy no longer recognized. Fortunately, despite massive police intervention, attempts to force a return to the classrooms met with failure. Predictably, several months into the strike, the students mobilized on a very large scale to defend not just their strike, but more fundamentally, their dignity as citizens. The strong-arm tactics failed, but they shed a stark light on a certain elite's conception of democracy.

The offensive against student democracy culminated with the idea that it was not "in the street" but "at the ballot box" that the political direction of Quebec should be decided. In the spring of 2012 it became clear that democracy, for many people, comes down to a private and passive activity: voting in secret, preferably not too often, no more than once every four years. Based on this line of reasoning, electronic voting – the possibility of voting with no clothes on in the privacy of one's bedroom and insulated from any encounter with others – would be the highest expression of citizenship. It would represent the attainment of a sort of ideal of political conservatism: democracy without the people, or a collective life free of the "hell" of having to deal with others. Yet, in the well-turned words of the political philosopher Jacques Généreux, "No one can be, or once again become, a citizen where the community no longer exists."[6] Our lives and rights as individuals are real only because they are recognized by others and socially and collectively guaranteed. The toads that prefer stagnant swamp waters and live in fear of spring floods may not like the idea, but debates, political conflicts, and the "street" are not the foes of political freedom, but its very lifeblood.

Agoraphobia, the term used by the political scientist Francis Dupuis-Déri to describe such anti-democratic views, is the product of a twofold reduction: first, of politics to parliamentary democracy; and second, of parliamentary democracy to elections. Through this reductive process, democracy is subjected to the will of the government, which is entitled to enact its decisions without restraint until the following election. This was precisely the argument that was marshalled to discredit the student protests. As of April 20, the editorialist André Pratte called on the government to crush the movement and to refuse all negotiations with the students' representatives, adding that "in this case, firmness is not obstinacy; it is simply governing."[7] A few weeks later, Mr. Pratte offered this advice to the students: "In short, the students should go back to their courses and transfer their mobilization from the streets to the ballot boxes."[8] I soon stopped counting the number of times the media dished out that argument: instead of demonstrating, go vote in the elections! The poverty of this conception of democracy is astounding, even for Liberals. One need not be a revolutionary to concede that democracy is not confined to the election process. Alexis de Tocqueville, a nineteenth-century writer whom no one would seriously associate with the far left, wrote that democracy was also and especially a social state characterized by the dynamic participation of citizens in every aspect of collective life, in particular through all sorts of political associations.

There is a glaring irony inherent in the statements of those who, from the commanding heights of their editorial authority, called on the government to turn a deaf ear to the strident "minority" known as the *carrés rouges* – that is, the bearers of the red square insignia. Once again, André Pratte of *La Presse*: "Why should Quebec City submit to the wishes of the university students, a privileged social group if ever there was one?"[9] One is tempted to ask in return: "Why should the government in Quebec City submit to the wishes of businessmen, university principals, and editorialists of the mainstream newspapers, a privileged social group if ever there was one?" Moreover, if those demanding that the government refuse to dialogue with the students were to act even minimally in accordance with their stated positions, they would immediately stop writing editorials. Because, if one reduces democracy to the electoral game and to the decisions made by the victors, then there is no point whatsoever in carrying on a public debate between elections. The student movement was accused of engaging in a trial of strength with the government to force it to retreat on a decision made through democratic procedures. But isn't this exactly what many commentators at *La Presse* and the *Journal de Montréal*[10] do all the time, especially when the government happens to adopt progressive measures? Didn't they rush to the aid of the wealthiest citizens when the government of Pauline Marois wanted to increase their income tax rates in the fall of 2013? Students, teachers, nurses, indeed nearly the whole middle class, not to mention the poor, often resort to noisy methods in their attempts to sway those in power. They go on strike, they yell, and sometimes they even get angry. They should be forgiven, because when they want to be heard they do not have at their disposal the more refined resources of an editorialist or the powerful resources of a media corporation.

In the discourse of the politicians, and even within the student movement, the direct democracy practiced in social movements is all too often set in opposition to institutional politics. This is a mistake. The day the election was called in August 2012, the then premier Jean Charest, playing on this false opposition, stated, "There has been a lot of noise coming from the streets. Now Quebeckers will have a chance to speak and to decide how the issues will be resolved." The fact is, however, that these are not two separate worlds. The whole history of the twentieth century, specifically in Quebec, is made up of struggles waged by ordinary people, trade unionists, students, and feminists, who, through an ongoing interaction with those wielding political power, achieved advances in the living conditions of the people of Quebec. Through social movements, a large portion of the population takes part in political life and expresses its views; this is in no way comparable to lobbyism, which strives to ensure that those holding political power will continue to serve strictly private interests. In other words, the "street" can hardly be blamed for eroding democracy. On the contrary, it is an integral and essential component of democracy, and a democratic government is duty-bound to dialogue with it – that is, with those affected by government decisions.

Just like unions and community groups, student associations belong to the space of discussion that serves, among other things, as a check on power, no matter how democratic that power may be. There is a wide gap between individuals and state power, and democracy needs intermediate stages to link them together; such stages are where we learn to care about the specific issues affecting our existence, where we become committed to confronting those issues and to integrating them into the whole of society. A free society is strengthened, not weakened, by the number and diversity of spaces of political participation that enable individuals to eventually deal with collective, often abstract, issues.

Such are the findings, supported by statistical evidence, of the American economist Paul Krugman, winner of the 2008 Nobel Prize in his field. In the United States, he explains, the strength of the union movement clearly fostered more political awareness and participation among low- and middle-income Americans. He cites a recent analysis showing that had the percentage of unionized workers among the active population been the same in 2000 as it was in 1964, the proportion of adults who voted in elections would have been 10 per cent greater among the lowest-earning two-thirds of the population, but only 3 per cent greater among the highest-earning third. For Krugman, the current disinterest in public affairs stems from the widespread feeling among average workers that their individual vote does not matter, even if the election outcome directly affects their lives. "People with jobs to do and children to raise have little incentive to pay close attention to political horseraces. In practice, this rational lack of interest imparts an upward class bias to the political process. . . . As a result, the typical *voter* has a substantially higher income than the typical *person*, which is one reason politicians tend to design their policies with the relatively affluent in mind."[11] By urging workers to go vote and, especially, by promoting political education and citizen involvement in union organizations, trade unionism helps to close that gap: "The discussion of politics that takes place at union meetings, the political messages in mailings to union members, and so on, tend to raise political awareness not just among union workers but among those they talk to, including spouses, friends, and family."[12]

Krugman's observations can easily be applied to the Quebec student movement, whose historic strike in 2012 invigorated democracy by politicizing hundreds of thousands of people. Even those who later paraded in the streets banging on pots and pans in defiance of the special law, Law 78, did not thoughtlessly reject political authority in favour of the "street." In fact, they were defending the rule of law against an arbitrary abuse of legislative power. They were expressing their profound attachment to democracy. The strike, including the assemblies and the pots-and-pans movement that marked its high point, was the best school of political involvement that one can imagine. I have no doubt that it served democratic culture better than did the Liberals, their financial backers, and their mainstream media cheerleaders.

Two Notions: "Fair Share" and "Excellence"

{ Four }

The Revolt of the Rich

When men cannot change things, they change the words.
— Jean Jaurès

Thanks to the Liberals, we learned at least one thing during the strike: words are important enough for some people to take pains to distort their meaning. "Students must do their fair share." Line Beauchamp, then minister of education, and her colleagues repeated this mechanically throughout the strike. It was their substitute for thought, inasmuch as such a statement deserves that title. Admittedly, the Liberals, or the PR firm they hired, had come up with a formidable slogan. The "fair share" message was simple, easy to remember, and smothered in "good common sense." Who could be against everyone doing his or her fair share? No one, of course. Yet there is something incredibly arbitrary about this proposition. What fairness and what share are we talking about when university tuition fees are raised by $1,625?

The "students' share" of university financing has varied considerably over the past forty years. Between 1970 and 1990, successive governments froze tuitions and increased education funding, so that by the end of the 1980s university fees were almost zero. In 1988 students paid 5.4 per cent of the cost of their post-secondary education, but by 2012 their share had risen to 14 per cent.[1] As it happens, the vast majority of the Charest cabinet members had received their diplomas during the earlier period. Line Beauchamp graduated in 1985, shortly before Julie Boulet, and Jean Charest received his law degree in 1981, the same year that his colleagues Pierre Moreau and Jean-Marc Fournier graduated from university.[2] Had they done their fair share? Not according to their own standards of fairness.

The universities attended by these government leaders were made accessible by funds provided through the income taxes on their parents' economic activities. They belong to the most educated generation in the history of Quebec, thanks largely to very low tuition fees. Now, however, they refuse to pay comparable income taxes that would make the universities accessible to the next generation. They are reneging on a social contract and, by way of justification, they have invoked a new idea of fairness resting on three principles: higher tuition fees, now regarded as the "fair share" that individuals must pay; indebtedness, regarded as a personal investment; and the sharing of costs, but not of wealth.

Though not often underlined, it is a remarkable fact that some major figures of the former power elite wholeheartedly supported the students' cause: Guy Rocher, Jean Garon, Jean Cournoyer, Jacques Parizeau, Lise Payette, and Jacques-Yvan Morin[3] all came out in favour of the principle of free university education. Unlike those currently in power, they understand from experience the social impact of restricting access to higher education. Together they have argued that it actually would be *un*fair to deprive people of an education for monetary reasons – that "the fee hike is not necessary"[4] (Jean Garon); that "free tuition is realistic"[5] (Jacques Parizeau); and that education is a "collective value as much as an individual one"[6] (Guy Rocher). Meanwhile, Lise Payette spoke out "as a woman who was prevented from pursuing the education she wanted because her parents were poor and she was a girl."[7]

These individuals are defending a conception of "fair share" and public service that is poles apart from the one held so dear by the political leaders now in office. During the strike, each in his or her own way recalled the spirit that has guided the universities of Quebec for fifty years, and that the Parent report[8] described in these terms: "The social benefits of a university education weigh more heavily than the individual benefits." They have maintained that education is not just a lever for personal gain, but also a social institution. This is the idea that has governed the edification of the public university system in Quebec for fifty years. Otherwise, education would not have been one of the cornerstones of the collective emancipation project known as the Quiet Revolution.

These political personalities, who indeed built the current system, are aware of another important historical and sociological truth: access to education was crucial for the development of a middle class in Quebec. The education reform that was propelled by the publication of the Parent report was part of a wide-ranging plan of social transformation whose most significant achievement was to lay down the institutional basis for a middle-class society. At the time, the saying *"S'instruire c'est s'enrichir"* – "Education brings enrichment" – was understood in both individual and collective terms. It was all interrelated. Wage earners knew that they had everything to gain as individuals when they defended themselves as a group, through trade unions, institutions, and political action. In addition, for francophones, it was obvious that economic independence was a collective issue of the highest order, because the other forms of independence – cultural, social, and political – are contingent upon it. With this in mind, everyone, including the Liberals of Jean Lesage, saw free education as a sound policy, one that was necessary to improve the living conditions of the majority of the population and essential in order to realize the great idea of that time: to become *maîtres chez nous* – masters of our own house.

The tuition freeze enacted in Quebec in the late 1960s was intended as a *transitional* measure toward the goal of free education, a goal the current political and economic elite has lost sight of so completely that it can no longer wrap its collective head around the idea of a tuition freeze. I clearly remember a debate with Luc Godbout, a well-known economist at the Université de Sherbrooke and a strong advocate of a tuition increase. He contended that the principle of freezing tuition fees had to be put aside because, as the expression goes, "everything costs more," so a freeze would amount to gradually reducing the students' participation in university funding and proportionally increasing the state's participation.

My response was that his reasoning was correct, but it glossed over one important point: it was in order to achieve precisely the result he described that tuition fees had been frozen for so long.

A tuition freeze is beyond the grasp of the facile bookkeeping mentality of Luc Godbout, Raymond Bachand, and company. Yet it has always seemed sensible, certainly to those who are concerned about keeping the universities open to the underprivileged members of society, but also to the daughters and sons of middle-class families, whose household incomes are by no means astronomical. In a study published in 2010, the FEUQ showed that 50 per cent of undergraduate students come from households whose yearly incomes are less than $65,000, a fraction of the income of those who claim to speak on their behalf.

It has often been said that the strike went much further than the sole matter of tuition fees. As the weeks passed, it brought together a host of political hopes, from the very moderate to the most radical, and gave vent to the myriad frustrations caused by a thoroughly corrupt government, until it ultimately transformed into a "social crisis." Rivers of ink were devoted to the topic of the "crisis," primarily to its intensity, its "violence," and its "chaos." There was a good deal of handwringing about the fears and exasperations that the crisis engendered for the public. Yet precious little thought was given to the adjective used to describe the crisis: "social." Consequently, one avoided the question of which group, within the fabric of Quebec society, so forcefully opposed the policies of the *lucides*, the so-called "clear-sighted ones" – policies centred on the imposition of exorbitant user fees. To all appearances, it was the part of society for which the "social benefits" of education always exceed the individual benefits: the middle class, wage earners, and the poor. Another reason for the magnitude of the student strike is that the people of Quebec set great store by the *institutional conditions* allowing the middle class to exist. It was not just choices, values, or personal convictions that were at stake, but something visceral and existential, because without those institutions, working people are at great risk.

Studies have demonstrated that over the past twenty-five years, Quebec families have found it harder and harder to stay in the middle class on the sole strength of "market" revenues, that is, income resulting from employment, business, and investment. Simon Langlois, a sociologist at Université Laval, has marshalled statistical evidence to show that "if one were to rely on the market alone, the proportion of households belonging to the middle classes would have shrunk from one third to one quarter of all households between 1982 and 2008."[9] What has prevented this from happening and kept the level of inequality in terms of disposable income relatively stable in Quebec is the redistribution of wealth through state mechanisms, specifically progressive income tax rates and transfers to families. This has been confirmed by the Institut de la statistique du Québec (Statistics Institute of Quebec): "Each year, market revenues contribute to inequality, while income tax and income from transfers contribute to equality, in keeping with their normal income redistribution function. [The] reduction of inequality has resulted strictly from those two factors, given that the market factor has contributed instead to increasing the level of inequality during this period."[10] In sum, without the progressive fiscal policy typical of the Quebec socio-economic model, families here would have become significantly poorer between the late 1970s and the 2000s. They likely would have shared the fate of families in the US, whose assets and freedoms have both been severely eroded over the past thirty-five years.

Education also plays an important role in developing and maintaining the middle class. Today's middle-class families are more educated than they were in 1982.[11] There are two reasons for this. First, among the active population of the 1980s, most of those with a post-secondary education had graduated at the end of the 1950s, a time when few individuals went to university, largely because major education reforms were still some years down the road. Second, since the 1980s, education has become an increasingly significant factor in social mobility. Note that between 1945 and 1975, less educated workers saw their wages go up around 100 per cent, but since the 1980s, wages have stagnated or even decreased in some cases.

If, as Jean Garon rightly observed during the student strike, the tendency to follow the US model is not halted, "the middle class will pay the price."[12] The Quebec model has its shortcomings, but the neoliberal economic policies of the last fifteen years have been pushing wage earners and their families to the brink of a social abyss. Yet recent governments have claimed to be acting in their interest (equated with lightening the "tax burden") whenever they have introduced austerity measures and privatized public institutions. No one has explained that workers' standard of living is maintained through taxes and public services, so they deduce that lowering taxes will make them individually richer. Based on this logic of "everyone for him or herself," the principle of free (in this case) tuition funded through taxation is turned into an injustice, and a "fair share" becomes what individuals should pay to finance the public services that they use. That was exactly the position taken by Jean-François Lisée[13] when he objected to the fact that a business person with just a high-school diploma could end up paying for the university education of the daughter of a couple of doctors. From this self-centred perspective, raising tuition fees would relieve the taxpayer of the burden of having to pay for universities, whose operations will benefit their graduates first and foremost. This view of society is presented as altogether natural, whereas it represents a radical break with the principles and institutions that have forged the identity and soul of modern Quebec.

Far more than a response to "economic" necessities or a mundane management issue, the rightward shift of recent years is the Quebec version of "the revolt of the rich" that has afflicted the United States for the last thirty-five years. Even the multi-billionaire investor Warren Buffett has admitted that his country is the scene of a class struggle that has been waged and won by his camp. One need only listen to CHOI-FM[14] or look at a copy of the *Journal de Montréal* to be convinced. Welfare recipients, trade unionists, intellectuals, artists, and students are accused of being responsible for the putative economic sluggishness of Quebec. Listeners and readers are emphatically asked to stand behind the great barons of the business world in their efforts to "kick-start Quebec." Appeals are made to "individual responsibility," and the middle class is recruited into a "crusade against taxes,"[15] which is nothing but a war against what those taxes pay for: education, public health services, pensions, culture – in a word, everything that has prevented the Quebec middle class from going downhill in recent years. The very rich have understood that as a group they have everything to gain from persuading us that we exist only as individuals.

The extent of the media mobilization preceding the 2010 announcement of the tuition fee hikes was staggering. Between 2005 and 2010, out of 143 columns and editorials dealing with the issue, only four were opposed to the increase.[16] Clearly, without the strike, without the economic disruption actions, without the people in "the street" – their freedom of expression, their spontaneity, even their radicalism – Quebec would never have had a debate on the reorientation and reorganization of the universities. Never. Only one discourse would have been heard in the public arena, claiming to represent a consensus. It therefore would have been considered altogether normal for university graduates, thanks to a diploma that generally ensures them a higher income, to pay more for their education. Accordingly, Youri Chassin of the Institut économique de Montréal compared a university degree to a "lottery ticket that is always a winner." In one of a series of video clips broadcast at the start of the strike to convince students of the tuition hike's legitimacy, Education Minister Line Beauchamp took up that very same line of argument. Over the course of their careers, she affirmed, university graduates would earn on average $750,000 more than those with just a high-school diploma. An investment of $1,625 that yields $750,000 – who could refuse an offer like that, even if it meant going into debt to the tune of tens of thousands of dollars? If not for the strike, Quebec as a whole ultimately, and unwittingly, would have come to see education as an "investment" in one's "human capital" in exchange for a future salary.

The concept of human capital is used by economists and university authorities as a *descriptive* term, one that is believed to adequately describe the true motive for student behaviour. Guy Breton[17] thus stated in January 2012 in *Le Devoir* that "people do not want to study for the sake of studying. They study in order to get work."[18] The French sociologist Christian Laval has observed that this argument is egregiously circular: since individuals with the most education generally earn a better salary, it can be inferred that this is the only motivation for studying. In reality, however, young people enter university for a variety of reasons. Some do it because they are passionate about a certain subject, others out of intellectual curiosity, while still others have their sights set on a specific profession, which may or may not be lucrative. But raising tuition fees is a surefire way of restricting their freedom, because the prospect of entering the labour market weighed down by a heavy debt load is bound to constrain students' thinking. Faced with a debt of tens of thousands of dollars, they will be attracted to programs that lead to high-paying jobs, enabling them to pay off their loans more quickly and thereby improve the yield on their "investments." So the concept of human capital as a justification for increasing tuition fees is in fact a *self-fulfilling prophecy*. Far from describing what is, it points to what should be.

The problem with these theories on human capital, to borrow from Hannah Arendt's view on behaviour theories, "is not that they are wrong but that they could become true."[19] The notion of human capital underpinning the tuition increase is in reality *prescriptive* – one more disastrous project promoted by the Western elites, but one that fortunately has been met with much resistance along the way. And no wonder! Who would willingly comply with such a notion? Student debts are paid back not just in capital and interest, but also at the cost of changing one's behaviour, adapting one's lifestyle, and modifying one's tastes and interests.[20] They have a powerful disciplinary effect on people and drastically restrict their freedom. Noam Chomsky argues that students who accrue large debts are generally not inclined to turn their thoughts toward social change. "When you trap people in a system of debt, they can't afford the time to think,"[21] he says. Chomsky describes tuition fee increases as a "disciplinary technique," and notes that by the time they graduate, students are not just burdened with debt but have also internalized "the disciplinarian culture," making them excellent consumers.[22] The pressure of being in debt leads students to integrate performance requirements into their relationships with others; it induces them to value only their economic potential, to think of their actions only in terms of efficiency and profitability, and therefore to stifle their callings, their talents, and their intellectual curiosity. Having turned themselves into veritable business projects, indebted students develop potential markets and find valuable contacts; they expect the university to become a site for "networking"; they manage their personal schedules as efficiently as possible and juggle the increasingly conflicting, but profitable, demands of gainful employment with those of formal learning; they look upon their colleagues with suspicion and will go to any lengths to obtain the best possible grades.

"Economics," as Margaret Thatcher so aptly put it, "are the method"; the aim is to change souls. Raymond Bachand boasted that the tuition fee hikes would usher in a veritable "cultural revolution." But the former minister of finance was careful to omit that what he sought to overthrow was the social order of the middle class, which had at least one virtue: it tried to free people from economic need.

o o o

Some clever minds will retort that there is ample leeway between free tuition and the fees required by, say, Harvard University. The state can very well assist individuals-entrepreneurs-investors, just as it supports legal entities such as large corporations. This was the sort of "compromise" that we were offered. In other words, bend your principles and a safety net will be set up for the less fortunate. Oh, great!

If you want to know what happens when you sell your soul to the devil, just consider the events in the land of Mrs. Thatcher. While visiting Paris in December 2012, I was able to meet with Claire Callender of the Higher Education Institute at the University of London, an expert on issues of access to higher education. The fact is that the UK is a genuine laboratory in the area of tuition fees. Between 1998 and 2012, through a series of reforms, the country went from free tuition to one of the world's most "advanced" education systems in terms of privatized funding.

As I write, the last of these reforms has just been implemented. It is an interesting plan insofar as it includes most of the items advocated on this side of the Atlantic by "clear-sighted" think tanks like the IEDM. The British government is raising the upper limit of tuition fees to £9,000 (around $17,000).[23] Below that ceiling, universities are free to set the rates for each of their programs; this amounts to a quasi-deregulation very similar to what the right wing in Quebec has been clamouring for. Note that all students, no matter their personal or family incomes, are eligible for loans covering the total cost of their university education. In other words, students pay zero tuition while they are studying; they can live, as it were, on borrowed time. Once they graduate, the loans are to be paid back in proportion to each student's income. It is estimated that students earning more than £21,000 will devote around 9 per cent of their annual income to paying down their debts. Interest rates can vary marginally, but will never be more than 3 per cent above the increase in the cost of living – that is, generally lower than the normal rates. In addition to this universal loan program, there is a vast supplementary program of subsistence loans, with the same terms of repayment. The government is also offering a generous scholarship program, with somewhat more restrictive eligibility criteria. Finally, another national program grants substantial scholarships on merit to students from underprivileged environments.

If one follows the line of argument maintained by the champions of the tuition fee hike in Quebec, the British government has come up with an ideal reform. Deregulation makes it possible to increase university funding and at the same time closely tie the cost of a diploma to its value on the job market, while fostering competition among the various institutions. What's more, the open-handed loan and scholarship program provides anyone wanting to obtain a university degree with the means to do so. Accessibility, performance, quality – the picture appears to be perfect. But that is a far cry from reality. I myself was surprised by the extent of the damage caused by this reform.

The initial results of Claire Callender's research are disturbing. For the 2012–13 academic year – barely a year after the new system was introduced – the number of admissions to universities in the UK had already dropped by an average of 10 per cent, which represents fifty-seven thousand fewer students in one year. For older students, the drop is even more severe: between 15 per cent and 20 per cent. According to Professor Callender's statistical projection, a further 10 per cent drop could be expected in 2013–14. The cumulative decline can only be described as dramatic.

The British experience highlights the strong connection between tuition fees and university enrolment.[24] Ingenious arrangements like those developed in the UK, which were applauded by the OECD, or even those imagined by Jean-François Lisée make no difference in this regard. The simplicity of free tuition, its proven benefits, both economic – for the middle class – and cultural, its effect on souls, to borrow Margaret Thatcher's terminology, are such that there is no good reason to dispense with it.

One could argue that tuition fees are not the only factor affecting enrolment in higher learning institutions. The priority that parents attribute to education, for instance, also plays a major role in a young person's decision to pursue a university degree. I agree. In fact, the cost of tuition may not even be the primary factor. What seems obvious, however, is that it is the only factor that we can act upon through political means. Hence the vigorous political debates on university accessibility that are presently underway worldwide: in China, Chile, the United Kingdom, Quebec, and even the United States.

So I will venture a prediction here: we have not heard the last of student movements.

{ Five }

Excellence?

If stupidity did not look so exactly like progress, talent, hope, or improvement, no one would want to be stupid.
— Robert Musil

In May 2012, as the strike grew more and more intense, a group of well-known personalities signed a letter in *Le Devoir* asking the state to signal that recess was over. The signees urgently called for an authoritarian gesture: "Order must be restored. The students must go back to school." The government, evidently not indifferent to every demand, answered their plea two weeks later by tabling Law 78. The letter was signed by the usual birds of evil omen, those who ritually predict the decline of Quebec, the failure of the state, and the bankruptcy of all public services: Joseph Facal, Lucien Bouchard, Michel Audet, Monique Jérôme-Forget, Claude Montmarquette, Yves-Thomas Dorval, Robert Lacroix.[1] These guardians of the conservative economic orthodoxy titled their missive "Universities – The Need for Excellence."[2] The appeal to excellence had become a recurring theme for the supporters of a substantial increase in tuition fees, as though the cost of education was the proper expression of its value. Excellence? Sure. But one wonders what these appeals to excellence are really worth, and, more importantly, if they are not actually a smokescreen for mediocrity.

What does "the university of excellence" refer to? Bill Readings, a former professor at the Université de Montréal, provides an illuminating answer to this question in his book *Dans les ruines de l'université*.[3] Today, he explains, excellence has replaced culture and reason as the ultimate goal of academic activity. This new objective, which is both flashy and vacuous, is the keyword for universities left to fend for themselves in the global education market. The university of excellence has cut itself off from its national context, repudiated the legacy of modernity, and thereby abandoned its original objective: to bring the culture of a people into the global conversation of humankind.

The French philosopher Jacques Derrida, who certainly cannot be accused of conservatism, offers an accurate description and a cogent defence of the classic university model, currently in jeopardy:

> The modern university *should* be without condition. By "modern university," let us understand the one whose European model, after a rich and complex medieval history, has become prevalent, which is to say "classic," over the last two centuries in states of a democratic type. This university claims and ought to be granted in principle, besides what is called academic freedom, an *unconditional* freedom to question and to assert, or even, going still further, the right to say publicly all that is required by research, knowledge, and thought concerning the *truth*. . . . It declares and promises an unlimited commitment to the truth.[4]

One need only listen to the speeches of the rectors of Quebec universities to realize that none of those virtues – neither the "unlimited commitment to the truth," nor the "unconditional freedom to question" – enters into their concept of the excellence they claim to cultivate in their establishments. Judith Woodsworth, the former rector of Concordia University,[5] made clear what she meant by "the need for universities of excellence" in an address to a meeting of business people held by the Canadian Club of Montreal:

> As head of a university establishment, I would like to draw your attention to the huge potential of our universities. I want you to think of us as *engines of economic development and centres of intellectual entrepreneurship*, endowed with the skills and know-how needed to

meet the challenges of both society and the economy. I am therefore asking you to act and *to help us help you.* Come to our defence, take part in our research, hire our graduates, and support our efforts to obtain better funding. Society as a whole will benefit from this. But we must do more. We have neglected to maintain and develop the human and intellectual capital of our post-secondary institutions.[6]

In concluding her enthusiastic talk, Woodsworth, on behalf of all Montreal universities, deplored how slow Quebec society was to take hold of the "powerful resource" that universities represent in order to meet its "economic and social challenges." On October 5, 2012, her counterpart at the Université de Montréal, Guy Breton, offered a foretaste of the consequences of this new orientation. The occasion was the very exclusive Rendez-vous du savoir (Rendezvous of knowledge), sponsored by, among others, the Montreal Council on Foreign Relations. Henceforward, he stated bluntly, "brains must coincide with the needs of businesses." The classic university, rooted in the Enlightenment, required "unconditional freedom" and dreamed of well-rounded minds. Guy Breton dreams of a university that provides just-in-time delivery of brains to the marketplace.

For a number of years, the rector of the Université de Montréal has been elected by a board made up mostly of private-sector actors. This practice is referred to as "good governance" and involves formally separating the bureaucracy from faculty, students, and employees. On one hand the decision-makers, on the other the workers who keep the brain mill running. During the strike, the extent to which the relations between the administration and the university community had deteriorated was plain to see. In order to obtain an interlocutory injunction banning political demonstrations from the Université de Montréal premises, the management lawyers did not hesitate to argue before the Quebec Superior Court that the campus was private property, "just like a shopping centre." The administration deemed it legitimate to forbid any action that might impede the normal activities of its "shopping centre." Consequently, many university departments called for police assistance to force professors to give their courses. This gave rise to some surreal moments: armed police ordering professors to teach and security guards yelling at lecturers to go to their classes. At the Université du Québec en Outaouais, a professor who had gone to fetch a book in his office was detained and accused of hindering a police officer in the performance of his duties. It would appear that the rectors' version of excellence will not come into the world naturally, but will have to be brought in by force.

The word *university* derives from the Latin *universitas*, meaning "turned toward unity," which suggests that the institution aims to form a community of scholars and that learning is always done with others. The term alludes to the universal and denotes an interest in all areas of knowledge. The bureaucrats who now manage our universities have, for all intents and purposes, turned their backs on these principles and are indifferent to the university community. By physically coercing professors into providing their "clients" the "services" they were paid to deliver, the rectors behaved like foremen determined to press their workers to the utmost and keep the "mill" running smoothly so as to maintain the graduation rate, which is the touchstone of excellence.

Fortunately, universities have not been turned into sausage plants. Intelligence has kept its rightful place there, and so has fundamental research. Nor can the students be admonished for wanting nothing but a good job once they graduate. But it would be ingenuous to believe that the rectors' commercial discourse has no effect on the culture. One would have to be in denial not to recognize the profound changes now at work in the institution. We must take stock of the upheaval that the advent of the university of excellence represents. The privatization of knowledge, the intrusion of quantity into the realm of quality and of greed into the domain of disinterested examination, the takeover of the institution by bureaucrats, the commodification of diplomas, the transformation of students into clients, the reduction of teachers to mere employees – all this bespeaks a coherent plan carried out in the name of, but to all appearances in the absence of, excellence. There is nothing in it that coincides with the ancient Greek idea of *arete*, meaning "excellence of any kind"; this was the virtue they valued above all others, and it referred to the correspondence between a thing and its raison d'être, its purpose. The bow and the horse were each thought to have their own forms of excellence. For humans, it implied effort and the ability to elevate oneself, to exercise and develop all one's aptitudes, especially those that encompass all the others: knowledge and wisdom. Today, as we have seen, the term *excellence* involves replacing the cultural ideals or aims of education with the logic of self-interest and money.

The founders of the modern university born of the Enlightenment drew upon the works of philosophers such as Kant, Herder, and Humboldt in defining the organization and social objective of the institution. It was the embodiment of a powerful idea. The contemporary university of excellence, in contrast, is an enterprise whose function is to produce graduates; it is a university centred on its own bureaucracy and whose greatest claim to glory is presumably to be a faithful servant to the economy. This university, which boasts of being open to the world – open, that is, to the global education market – is actually wrapped up in itself, having no points of reference to assess its efficiency other than its own operations. This vacuum is what is called *excellence*, and its yawning depths are sounded with performance indicators: graduation rates, donations to foundations, business ties, inter-university sports championships, number of Nobel prizes, amount of grants obtained, and so on. The only thing missing in this economic masquerade, with its student-consumers, its diploma-commodities, and its advertising spaces, is an exchange or a rating agency that would set the value of each school on the knowledge market. Welcome to the worldwide hit parade of universities.

For Bill Readings, excellence is the ideal of the university fallen under the sway of its bureaucrats and no longer able to define itself other than in terms of management (or, as today's newspeak would have it, governance). It is usually accompanied by the university's lack of ideas, or at least its lack of concern with developing ideas. The mandate of the rector, an administrator-bureaucrat, is confined to that of any business person: grooming the organization's image, elaborating "strategies for success," keeping the enterprise afloat, recruiting new clients, providing good service to the student-consumer, honouring the state's compulsory "performance contract" by producing graduates and delivering them to the marketplace on time, and attracting investors by supplying both a specialized workforce and researchers capable of enhancing their profits.

This, then, is the true context for the numerous scandals of poor management that have plagued Quebec universities. The modern university sought out the best thinkers and scientists, the best students, and it was censured whenever it became dogmatic. The university of excellence strives to find good administrators, and it is censured when it is mismanaged. On April 25, 2012, just after the failure of the first round of negotiations, a front-page article in the *Journal de Québec*[7] reported that the rectors of Quebec were leaving on a trip to Brazil organized by the Association of Universities and Colleges of Canada with the aim of recruiting new students. This was no shoestring operation. The renowned rector of McGill University, Heather Monroe-Blum, had asked to fly business class, at a cost of $9,470, not to mention the five-star hotel rooms in Rio de Janeiro and São Paulo. The rectors thus handed the student associations what looked like a watertight argument. For how could the university administrators dare to demand more from the students when they themselves were squandering their budgets on such indulgences?

Yet, while students cite such cases as examples of wasted university resources, the advocates of excellence tend to see them, on the contrary, as signs of good management. A rector who feels that her establishment must be competitive on the international higher-learning market has no reason to turn down a business trip aimed at finding new overseas outlets for her goods. Rather than being an extravagant expense, it is actually a sound investment. By the same token, it is an absolute necessity to put the university's administration in the hands of professional managers and technocrats. Far from being an instance of squandered funds, paying almost $500,000 a year to the rector of McGill University or granting the rector of Université Laval a $100,000 pay raise is regarded as perfectly normal.[8] To attract the best managers to our universities, one needs to offer competitive salaries. That is just the way things are for the super-elite of the global university system, where merit and quality are measured in hard cash.

That is why the striking student organizations had no qualms about denouncing the Quebec universities' misuse of public funds. All's fair in love and war. But taking this criticism too seriously can lead one down a slippery slope. In trying to defend the common good, one would actually end up adding a new component to the bureaucratic machinery of the university of excellence. There would be no benefit for teaching and research. During the strike, Martine Desjardins[9] repeatedly inveighed against the rectors for their "poor management"; however, though her criticism was not unjustified, she was aiming at the wrong target with her insistent calls for the creation of a "council of universities," as if a university were a head of lettuce whose freshness must be guaranteed by the state. What must be denounced is the bureaucratization of the university, not its bureaucrats; it is the cultural and intellectual imposture of the university of excellence, not its management. Even if tuitions were free, the university of excellence would be just as hollow, just as inane, only more democratically so. A victory of this sort would be a mirage, because the techno-bureaucratic monster that we have been fighting would thrive even more.

o o o

What the rectors' international junkets indicate is that the large-scale privatization of higher education is in no way specific to Quebec. It is a well-known fact that over the past number of decades the economies of developed countries have been transformed into economies of creation and conception, in tandem with the extensive delocalization of manufacturing activities to emerging countries. Biotechnology, pharmaceutics, telecommunications, microcomputers – these industries require a highly skilled workforce, high-tech facilities, and, most importantly, huge research and development investments in order to produce marketable results. They are costly and risky outlays that private companies hesitate to undertake. That is where the universities come in, as Mélanie Bourassa Forcier, a professor of pharmaceutical law at the Université de Sherbrooke, explains:

> It must be accepted that the pharmaceutical companies in Canada do not engage on their own in a great deal of innovation. This should not be frowned upon; they are private companies looking to make profits. It is up to us to see how we can profit from this kind of situation. And we need to understand that the companies can still be major investors in innovation, for example, at the marketing stage.[10]

In short, within this new dynamic, universities – financed through public funds and tuition fees – provide more and more subcontracted R&D services to private companies, which subsequently market the resulting products and, naturally, rake in the profits. In influential circles around the globe, it is readily affirmed that to remain competitive, developed countries must place their education systems at the service of the "knowledge economy." This new reality means that students are seen as clients by the university and as commodities by the companies claiming to invest in education. An OECD expert sums this up quite openly:

> Intelligence, when it is developed through education, in other words, *human capital*, is quickly becoming an essential economic resource, and this *imperative* gradually engenders an international education model. The member countries of the OECD expect their education systems and various professional training programs to play a major part in economic growth and they adopt the reforms that this requires.[11]

Our neighbours to the south are world leaders in this process. With the Bayh-Dole Act of 1980, the US became the first country to allow universities to patent the results of publicly funded research with a view to selling them to private interests. Private investments in university research immediately skyrocketed. Today, on the strength of this historic initiative, the United States is still in the vanguard when it comes to privatizing higher education establishments, as evidenced by the well-known university rankings, which consistently place Ivy League schools at the top.

In January 2013, the debate on university funding was in full swing in Quebec. In an unofficial comment made while the PQ-organized summit on the issue was underway, François Legault[12] expressed his gushing admiration for the American university model: "For me, the ideal is Silicon Valley, with Stanford and Berkeley nearby. That is the model that Quebec should follow. This doesn't mean doing away with general education, but simply banking on what is good for Quebec's economic development."[13] When rectors and business representatives talk about "shining among the best" or "competing with the top universities" or "improving the competitive position" of our universities, they want us to follow in the footsteps of those elite universities. But the advantage of living so close to the Americans – there must be at least one – is that we can more easily observe the cultural, social, and economic disaster resulting from the "university of excellence" project.

In *Empire of Illusion*,[14] the Pulitzer Prize–winning journalist Chris Hedges paints a frightening portrait of the model so admired by Mr. Legault. American universities, Hedges maintains, no longer encourage critical thinking but actively contribute to the ignorance and vast depoliticization of the American population.

The impact on academic freedom is calamitous. Noam Chomsky relates an anecdote about a computer science student who skipped over an exam question, to which he knew the answer, to avoid the risk of violating the secrecy that his research activities demanded.[15] In this case, Christian Laval observes, "the market value of research trumps its truth value . . . or, to put it another way, the truth, until now the bedrock of theoretical work, has been 'deconstructed' by the market."[16] In the race for private research funding, universities submit to the arbitrary authority of the economic powers they are courting. Such subordination can come at a high price. Ibrahim Warde reports that in the early 2000s the Nike Corporation suspended its financial support for the universities of Michigan and Oregon and for Brown University because students there openly protested against the multinational's practice of employing children in some countries.[17]

A correlation can also be established between tuition increases and the rise in student grade averages, something that Howard Hotson, president of the International Society for Intellectual History,[18] regards as a symptom of the clientelism spawned by exorbitant fees. No one dares to fail a "client" who has paid $15,000, or in some cases $50,000, in tuition fees. Meanwhile, the total student debt has gone through the roof, to the point where in 2011 *The Economist* feared that these loans would trigger the next financial bubble.[19] And this may indeed come to pass, for on March 22, 2012 – what a coincidence![20] – *Forbes* reported that the overall student debt in the United States had officially passed the trillion-dollar mark.[21] The economic crisis limits the income of graduates, and, given the poor "return on their investment," they struggle to pay back their loans.

All the fears expressed by Quebec students during their strike in 2012 have been borne out in the United States: imbalance among the various disciplines, attrition of faculty numbers, proliferation of managers, attacks on academic freedom, clientelism, lower academic standards, excessive indebtedness threatening economic stability, the strangling of the middle class. And this is the model that we are urged to import to Quebec!

As early as 1971, the sociologist Fernand Dumont succinctly framed the choice before us: "Either we turn our universities into poor imitations or ridiculous scale models of the most prestigious (or the wealthiest) neighbouring institutions, or we decide that our objectives must correspond to the fundamental intentions of learning and to [the needs of] a land such as this one."[22] The spring of 2012 reminded us that we had the option of not subscribing to the project of the university of excellence. The "all-for-the-market" ideology underpinning that project jeopardizes public education and imperils culture in general. For an uncompleted, culturally fragile land like Quebec, this avenue seems fraught with danger. Having identified the threat, one can plainly see the political inconsistency of independentists like Joseph Facal, Lucien Bouchard – assuming he is still a sovereigntist – or Mathieu Bock-Côté,[23] who support a project so harmful for the culture and identity of Quebec.

"American things will always be done best by Americans,"[24] the sociologist Marcel Rioux once remarked. The project referred to as "excellence" is culturally lethal and, at bottom, quite simply foolish: mimicking the mistakes of others has nothing to do with liberty or collective progress. Given the choice between the original and a copy, our fellow citizens always prefer the original. In 2012, the youth of Quebec endeavoured to expose the absurdity of the plan to denationalize the universities. Quebec has nothing to gain from such a scheme, other than the mediocrity and ignorance that are now clearly undermining the public sphere in the US.

Faced with this attempt to Americanize the Quebec education system, young adults have answered with an energetic defence of the principles inherited from the Quiet Revolution, which, though imperfect, nevertheless offered an effective compromise between the concern for public usefulness and the humanist, republican project of democratizing education. The cégeps continue to embody that project. The attacks against them are symptomatic of the looming threat to accessible education, the legacy of the hard-fought battles of the 1960s. Today, cégep administrators too are increasingly adopting the managerial mentality that is playing havoc with our universities. They regard the cégeps as service counters, and, under the impetus of performance incentives and all manner of strategic plans, they devote themselves entirely to producing graduates while sacrificing the quality of their education. Cégeps were created to combine technical and professional training with general knowledge and culture. It is therefore not surprising that François Legault should be so vigorously opposed to them. What is more worrisome is the growing number of cégep administrators and officials lining up behind him, as evidenced by their oft-expressed misgivings about mandatory philosophy courses.

There are those who claim that democratizing education necessarily entails the waning of intellectual refinement. Others insist that defending the classic university and humanist education is elitist and harks back romantically to the good old days of the *cours classiques*.[25] Granted, the modern university was an elite institution, and the contemporary university has opened its doors to the masses. But can its current cultural decline really be ascribed to the influx of plebeians, who some say are more concerned with feeding their bellies than nurturing their minds? Must the university's value diminish simply because it has accepted working-class people as students? If that were the case, one would have to admit that democracy itself is impossible, or that it can be no more than a process for choosing leaders, the only ones who know enough to manage society, as the American conservatives would have us believe.

It is wrong to say that we must choose between general education and democracy, between the freedom to know and social justice. The university's goal should not be to train, *at all costs*, the greatest possible number of people, and especially not to provide *just any sort of training*. The choice is not between the model of excellence promoted by today's rectors-cum-business-people, and that of the bygone elitist universities. Given the utter failure of the university as "pen-pusher-mill," to borrow the coinage of the defunct Association nationale des étudiantes et étudiants du Québec (Quebec national student association),[26] we now must conceive of a university that is accessible, free of charge, and free to pursue its universal calling, and that also provides solid professional training. This requires a good deal of courage and imagination of the sort displayed by young people in the spring of 2012, which suggests that it is in no way naive to believe that this alternative project can be realized in Quebec.

Part 3

A Struggle

{ Six }

Soldiers without a Commander?

At any given moment there is an orthodoxy, a body of ideas which it is assumed that all right-thinking people will accept without question. It is not exactly forbidden to say this, that or the other, but it is "not done" to say it, just as in mid-Victorian times it was "not done" to mention trousers in the presence of a lady. Anyone who challenges the prevailing orthodoxy finds himself silenced with surprising effectiveness. A genuinely unfashionable opinion is almost never given a fair hearing, either in the popular press or in the highbrow periodicals.

— George Orwell

On Monday, April 23, there was a flurry of events. The previous weekend, after much wavering, the convention of the CLASSE had adopted a resolution condemning deliberate physical violence against individuals while reaffirming the organization's support for the principles of civil disobedience. That morning, Minister Line Beauchamp's chief of staff, Philippe Cannon, announced to the CLASSE's negotiator, Philippe Lapointe, that we would be invited to the negotiating table. After waiting for months, the Liberal government had finally agreed to dialogue. At twelve noon, Line Beauchamp held a press conference. As she spoke, I was on hold with the Simon Durivage show on RDI,[1] where I was about to be invited to respond to the minister's remarks. In addressing the media, the minister asked the three pan-Quebec student associations to declare a forty-eight-hour "truce" to "allow a favourable climate for discussion to be established." Specifically, she demanded that we renounce all disruptive actions, but this did not include "traditional" demonstrations, which could continue. I was on a bus with the CLASSE's press agent, Renaud Poirier St-Pierre. We were watching the press conference on a cellphone. The minister's new demand took us by surprise, to say the least, because just three hours earlier her chief of staff had told us the invitation to the negotiations *was not subject to any conditions*. Was the minister genuinely committed to achieving the rapprochement the population was calling for?

My telephone interview with Simon Durivage began at 12:40 p.m. Naturally, he started by asking me if I accepted the truce. The question caught me off guard. I had been told that the minister would simply be announcing to the press our inclusion in the negotiations, so I had not consulted my executive about a possible but improbable government ultimatum. As spokesperson, I had been given a very specific job, which was to defend the convention's position in the public arena; this function did not carry with it any decision-making powers, either for me or for my colleague, Jeanne Reynolds.[2] At the CLASSE's weekly conventions, each student association belonging to the coalition had the right to speak and to vote; the decisions taken must be applied and defended by those acting at the national level, including the spokespersons. When the TV host asked me if I accepted the Liberal government's demand for a truce, I had been active in the student movement for four years and knew perfectly well that I was not empowered to give him an answer.

But I also knew that the official action plan adopted at the CLASSE convention did not provide for any disruptions or blocking actions within the next forty-eight hours. I therefore chose to extricate myself from this predicament by presenting the host with the unadulterated truth. Although I, in my capacity as spokesperson, was not authorized to declare a truce, I nevertheless could tell the public and the minister of education that the organization I represented was not planning any disruptions or blockades. To that extent, the truce was in effect de facto. The minister could rest assured: the negotiations would not be disturbed by any actions on the part of the coalition. It was plain to see that my reasoning annoyed Mr. Durivage. He repeated his question, and I repeated my response. This time he interrupted, accusing me of skirting the issue. On the contrary, I told him, my answer is very clear: the coalition is not planning any disruptive action during the time-frame set by Line Beauchamp, so the question of the truce is irrelevant. What would be the point of signing a ceasefire if there were no battle underway? His blunt reaction was to tell me to accept my responsibilities and stop being evasive. I tried to explain once again the constraints of being a spokesperson, at which point he simply hung up on me. I was aghast. This sort of treatment might have been expected from certain privately owned media, but from Radio-Canada? It was inconceivable. Hanging up on a guest? I turned to my press agent and described the interview. We were both appalled.

While Simon Durivage was giving me the business, Philippe Lapointe was busy calling Line Beauchamp's chief of staff to find out what their intentions were. He was reassured: the negotiations would indeed begin within a few hours. Despite my ambiguous on-air answer and my refusal to utter the minister's magic formula, negotiations between the government and the student associations would start that same day. My suspicions were confirmed: the demand for a truce had been nothing but an excuse to hold yet another press conference and to position the students as troublemakers; it had been staged to convince the public that the strikers alone were to blame for the social strife and "turmoil." Here was proof that the Liberal discourse about student "violence" was just a communications ploy, a pretence of moral indignation, probably planned long before the first student association had gone on strike.

That evening, new heights of absurdity were reached. Through the social networks, some Montreal activists organized a spontaneous march under the watchword "Fuck the truce"; it was one of the first nighttime marches. A few windows were broken along the way, and Line Beauchamp jumped at the chance to do a remake of the bad film of 2005. Back then, the government had negotiated only with the FEUQ and the FECQ, using violence as an excuse to exclude the least docile student organization (the CASSÉE).[3] The FECQ and the FEUQ ultimately settled the 2005 conflict by signing a questionable agreement, one that many strikers in fact rejected. The day after the nighttime demonstration, then, Line Beauchamp was quick to bar the CLASSE from the negotiating table, arguing that it had "violated the truce." The minister's little game was beyond ridiculous. Line Beauchamp was expelling us from the negotiations on the pretext that the demonstration held the previous night was posted on the calendar of the CLASSE's website – a public bulletin board, something very common on the web. She inferred from this that the coalition had promoted the event – which essentially amounted to organizing it – thereby violating a truce that we in fact had never signed. On top of this, the march that so vexed the minister had been held in protest at my response to Simon Durivage, which, some believed, verged on accepting the minister's ultimatum and therefore exceeded my mandate. "Fuck the truce" had in part been aimed at me.

The whole episode was a bit of second-rate burlesque. First, the call for a truce had been a show put on for members of the press corps, the only ones to believe it – no one had really asked the CLASSE to comply. Otherwise, our participation in the negotiations would not have been confirmed both before and after the minister's press conference. Second, how could we break a truce that we had never accepted? Not to mention that the rough stuff we were being blamed for had come in reaction to my stated positions.

These events unfolded at a time of growing anxiety among some segments of the population. It was becoming clear that the government's inertia in the face of the students' determination was leading Quebec down a blind alley. It was then that I took the full measure of the gap separating the CLASSE from the mainstream media and the world of traditional politics. I also realized that the Liberals would take advantage of the journalists' difficulty in understanding the strike and, especially, the workings of the CLASSE.

Throughout the strike, the coalition was taken to task for its slowness, its idealism, and its intricate procedures. Was it possible to respond to the government with such a cumbersome organization? Could decisions be made quickly when the representatives' hands were tied? The more polarized the conflict became, the greater the pressure on the CLASSE's structure; by degrees, the blame for the conflict getting bogged down was laid at my doorstep. For some, the crisis was heating up because I claimed not to have any power, because I refused to play a leadership role. Even those who supposedly knew and understood the CLASSE's organizational setup asked me, at one point or another, to "commit" myself and initiate a solution to the crisis.

It is telling that the political culture of the coalition gave rise to more public disapproval than Premier Jean Charest's cavalier attitude during the conflict. His government ignored the students for seventy-three days and then sought by all possible means to impede genuine negotiations, as his ministers engaged in rhetorical contortions to draw attention away from the real issues. All these fine people worked very hard to channel public debate into the gutter. Never mind, say the pundits, all's fair in love and war, including this sort of cynicism. Get over it, get real, they say. Denounce it? Don't be ridiculous. The CLASSE wanted to go to the heart of the matter, to debate the basic objectives of the university, to put back on the agenda the promise Quebec had made to itself forty years earlier: free university education. Some have depicted that commitment as radical and dogmatic; the Liberals, meanwhile, were busy launching a "cultural revolution," abandoning the principle of progressive taxation in favour of user pays, overhauling the principles of public administration, fleecing the middle class to deck out the wealthy. Under their administration, the entire body politic was infected by greed. Yet it was said that they were pragmatic, that Jean Charest and Co. acted responsibly; they had made a decision and were doing whatever it took to carry it out, as true leaders should. Whereas Jeanne Reynolds and I were remiss in our obligations because we refused to impose our views on the students and submitted every important issue, every crucial decision, to the democratic judgment of those concerned.

I remember an interview on French television (i.e., from France) with Antoine Robitaille, a journalist for *Le Devoir* and by no means a fool. When the interviewer asked his Québécois colleague to describe my personality, he explained that I needed a mandate in order to take a position on a given issue. Then Robitaille added, very naturally, that this was often Nadeau-Dubois's way of being evasive so as to skirt journalists' queries on difficult issues – for example, the question of violence. Rather than mentioning that my freedom to express my views was restricted by the highly democratic workings of the organization I represented, he stayed on the surface of things and chided me for having invented a new kind of doublespeak.

This supports the analysis articulated by Chantal Francoeur, who teaches journalism at UQAM. At the peak of the mobilization she told *La Presse*:

> I was struck by, among other things, the difficulty the media and journalists have in covering whatever does not fit into the usual boxes. Take the CLASSE, for instance. This association displays a different conception of democracy, which does not coincide with the one familiar to us. The problem is, how to cover it. Through the Web, it would have been possible to explain how it operates, instead of presenting it as a deviation from the norm.[4]

Expanding her analysis in a full study published several months after the end of the strike, Francoeur observed that journalists use specific formats to construct their articles, which generally are not adapted to original political phenomena, such as the CLASSE. Such "journalistic assembly lines" enable reporters to stage different actors on different topics while using the same format. The trouble is that the coalition was ill-suited to these rituals of media coverage:

> When an explanation is needed as to why, for example, the CLASSE cannot spontaneously denounce violence – because an appropriate motion would have to be passed at a student assembly, with the assembly taking place on such-and-such a date, bringing together such-and-such people, proceeding according to such-and-such criteria, and having spokespersons who are just spokespersons and must abide by a strictly defined mandate, etc. – there is a problem: the explanation does not fit into the journalistic formats.[5]

That is why my public position ended up being relayed by the media in these terms: "Gabriel Nadeau-Dubois refuses to condemn the violence." The statement was inaccurate. I had not refused to do so as an individual; I had tried to explain that to do so was not within my mandate as spokesperson. Journalists found this proposition too complex, too unusual. "Only two clips or quotes can fit into the journalistic formats," writes Francoeur. "Either 'the CLASSE refuses to condemn violence,' or 'the CLASSE condemns violence.' Neither of these propositions correlates with the reality of the CLASSE."[6] It was impossible for me to conform to this binary logic, and that was what put Simon Durivage's nose out of joint.

Léo Bureau-Blouin,[7] on the other hand, was the student leader best adapted to the communications mould and to the Manichean expectations of a political sphere dominated by public relations. He did not hesitate to condemn certain actions, to denounce civil disobedience, to call for injunctions to be respected, to openly wish for the conflict to be settled. He was the first to distance himself from the CLASSE, to ask young people to vote (for him!), to recommend acceptance of the government's offer; he was also the first student leader to appeal for a compromise and to intimate that the student movement might accept a reduced fee increase. Given all this, it was not surprising to see him move into parliamentary politics under the PQ banner. It has not been sufficiently pointed out, however, that while he was garnering brownie points from Mario Dumont, Liza Frulla,[8] and Mathieu Bock-Côté, his influence in the movement was waning. The more he claimed authority over the student movement and the more he complied with the political and media elites' unanimous wish for him to succeed in this regard, the weaker his actual ascendancy among the students grew. Not that the future PQ Member of the National Assembly (MNA) – later to be defeated in the 2013 provincial elections – lacked the necessary skills, but a large portion of the social movement was simply unwilling to be guided by leaders.

The gap between the expectations of the power and state elite and the strikers' frame of mind grew wider as the strike progressed. With each passing day, the demand that student leaders behave like military commanders on the battlefield was made more absurd by the spread of spontaneous actions and the strikers' increasing independence. It was precisely because Martine, Léo, Jeanne, and I were not "leaders" that the strike was so vigorous. What most observers of the 2012 student mobilization never understood was this: the movement was ungovernable, and this in fact contributed to its vitality, its dynamism, and its effectiveness.

Few people outside the student movement know that while I was being chastised in some quarters for refusing to lecture the strikers, I was being criticized within the coalition's coordinating structures for doing just the reverse. A number of times, student associations submitted censure motions against me, and some of them were passed. On at least one occasion, a motion was tabled to force me to give up my responsibilities. Several well-attended and lively general assemblies officially came out in favour of my dismissal on the grounds that I was being too free with the mandate I had received from the convention. There were complaints that some positions I had defended were too personal. CLASSE activists felt I took too much initiative; journalists, meanwhile, thought I was shirking my duties. A spokesperson's life is not so very different from that of a tightrope walker.

The CLASSE was the exact opposite of a monolith; in addition to the difficulty of getting the media to understand its workings, there was the difficulty of coping with its often stormy internal political dynamics. Most of the time, the resolutions adopted at the conventions were tenuous compromises resulting from long hours of tense debate, propositions framed at the eleventh hour to reconcile very sharp political disagreements. As spokespersons, Jeanne and I had not only to defend the organization but also to do it in a way that would raise as few hackles as possible among its different tendencies. While a great many members of the coalition acknowledged the importance of public debate – without which my job would have been meaningless – a significant fringe was flatly opposed to our presence in the mainstream media on the grounds that conventional forms of democratic conversation were essentially traps and that only by confronting the state head-on could we make any gains. This tendency carried enough weight within the CLASSE to seriously restrict my latitude.

From the very start, the mainstream media and many political analysts tried to explain the conflict of the spring of 2012 in terms of an ordinary "political matter" or a traditional labour dispute between an employer and unionized employees. And during the early weeks of the mobilization, that frame of reference was just about adequate. After all, here was a confrontation between the government and student bodies organized along "trade-union"[9] lines and presenting a concrete demand: cancel the 75 per cent university tuition increase planned for the following year. Besides, until around March 22, most of the marches and actions were coordinated by the three major pan-Quebec student organizations. Given this context, political observers could refer to the usual labour dispute categories to analyze the student mobilization; each action could be attributed quite readily to a specific organization, making it easier to interpret the action's significance. Also, with the weekly votes to renew the strike mandates in the cégeps and universities, it was possible to gauge the level of student support for the walkout and related actions. One could establish a chronology of the various demonstrations and observe the movement's progression so as to grasp its rhythm and predict its development, just as one would in an ordinary labour dispute. In sum, until March 22 the student strike still resembled what can be termed a "traditional" social movement, and to that extent it could be analyzed according to "traditional" political categories.

On March 22, the mobilization reached an initial peak. More than 300,000 out of 420,000 students were on strike, and close to 200,000 people marched together in the streets of Montreal. That day, the Liberal government let it be known through the media that it was not impressed by the demonstration. Far from abating, the mobilization actually gathered momentum. Thanks to social media, student networks expanded as never before, and independent actions were on the rise.[10] Meanwhile, a growing number of student associations adopted open-ended strike mandates. As of mid-April, the overwhelming majority of demonstrations and disruptive actions were organized on a completely decentralized basis by impromptu groups of individuals wishing to remain anonymous; this made it impossible – for the police, the media, and the CLASSE and its spokespersons – to know who was responsible for this or that action and exactly who or what was the target. With the proliferation of actions came a broadening of demands. The discourse on the ground grew more radical. The slogans evolved and hardened. Along with the tuition fee hike and the Liberal government, austerity policies, creeping commercialism in public institutions, and the destruction of nature through the unbridled exploitation of natural resources all came under attack. Even capitalism was condemned, an attitude that many considered as ludicrous as contesting the universal law of gravity. There was indeed a clamour rising from the streets in opposition to our economic system, and there were pundits and politicians ascribing this to the infiltration of the student movement by wicked individuals, extremists, and scum. To each historical period its heresy. In the Middle Ages, whenever non-believers challenged the authority of God, they were said to be possessed by the Devil. Nowadays, if a movement questions the benefits of Capital, it is suspected of being manipulated by raving lunatics.

For mainstream observers of the political game, things had gone beyond the familiar boundaries. How was one to resolve a conflict that was so . . . political? Many analysts and politicians could not bring themselves to accept that through the demonstrations the population was venting its very real disgruntlement; either that or they were simply incapable of understanding what motivated the marches. During interviews, I sensed that a wave of panic was taking hold of moderators and journalists. It was more than the media apparatus could handle. The "student conflict" was no longer mentioned; instead, the keywords were "social crisis," "mired," "loss of control," "chaos." It had to stop. Anxious outbursts stood in for analyses. The Liberals and their experts in hollow communications labelled that anxiety with a few phrases that were meant to explain everything, and they certainly caught on: "*les carrés rouges*," "the street," "violence and intimidation." The disturbances rather than the reasons for the social unrest gradually took over the public space.

Fears such as these, engendered by the uniqueness of the conflict and whipped up by the media, aggravated the misunderstandings as to my role. As the conflict intensified, my public persona increasingly became the catalyst for heated reactions, with more and more people demanding the impossible: essentially, that I put a damper on the situation. Subjected to severe criticism, under fire on every side for "my" refusal to condemn violence, I lived through the most trying moments of the strike, especially because the position adopted by the coalition did not coincide altogether with my own. At times I asked myself if I wanted my face, my name, my voice to continue to be associated with such confrontations and their inevitable excesses. The demonstration of April 20, held during the now famous Salon Plan Nord,[11] was particularly distressing for me. In the middle of an interview with Benoît Dutrizac, conducted while the demonstration was in progress, the interviewer informed me – on air – that paving stones had been hurled down onto the roadway of the Ville-Marie expressway. Of course, Dutrizac asked me the unavoidable question: Do you condemn these acts? This wasn't a matter of some overturned garbage cans or a few broken bank windows. The lives of innocent citizens had been endangered. I knew that I could not condemn the acts; the convention had not authorized me to do so. Yet at the same time I was deeply upset by what I had just learned. I could not endorse such acts. To my surprise, the host seemed to sense my discomfort. He let me skirt the question. As soon as the interview ended I called my colleagues in the executive. I was beside myself. I yelled, "This time it's gone too far!" After some discussion we agreed that we would risk going against the convention's mandate. The CLASSE would condemn these actions. The executive would defend me at the next convention, and, if need be, we would be recalled as a group. Ironically, the episode was soon forgotten. Some even claimed that the reprehensible acts had never been perpetrated, and I was never asked to condemn them publicly. Otherwise I would have done so unreservedly and with the support of the executive.

The pressure to which I had been subjected – being accused of not shouldering my "responsibilities as a leader" – made me doubt myself at several points throughout the strike. It was the philosopher Christian

Nadeau who, during one of our discussions, put my doubts to rest: "Your detractors were not interested in you because of your personal qualities, but only because of your position as spokesperson for the CLASSE. Now the same people are asking of you much more than can be expected of a spokesperson. That your personal qualities attracted a larger audience for what you had to say in no way alters the fact that your words were strictly determined by the mandate you received."

The reason some strikers identified with me was because I was among them and not above them. Certainly, that identification increased the pressure I felt, but it gave me no actual power. I worked with the media and did a good job, so I became a public figure as a matter of course. It was assumed that fame, on one hand, endowed me with some quasi-magical power over the crowds and, on the other hand, obliged me to bare my soul in public the way celebrities do. Had I listened to the voices telling me to give up my position as spokesperson, it would have been in exchange for a position as a "star." But I would have ended up representing no one but myself, like Paris Hilton. In other words, if I had chosen to stop speaking in the capacity of spokesperson, on what possible basis could I have spoken out? What on earth would my presence in the media have meant? Here is how Christian Nadeau summed up the situation: "If a spokesperson goes beyond what he is allowed to say – for example, by abusing his position to express his personal views – his message should not be deemed credible by the public. Essentially, a spokesperson has no more than a public face, contrary to a leader, who, like Janus, can have two faces, because he is invested with a twofold authority: the one he has over the movement he leads, and the one the movement he represents has over him."

Soldiers without a commander: that is what we in the CLASSE all were. And that is what scandalized those who were shocked by the happenings in the street.

{ Seven }

Collective Hysteria

Conscience, my dear fellow, is one of those sticks everyone takes
hold of to beat his neighbour but never uses on himself.
— Honoré de Balzac

April 21. I was in the CLASSE office and took a call from an activist in the Quebec City area. He frantically informed me that the *Journal de Québec* had published an article denouncing the CLASSE's affiliation with the anarcho-communist group Union Communiste Libertaire (UCL). At first I thought this was impossible, that he must have misread. But the newspaper's website confirmed his report. Under the title "Les Soviets de salon" ("Armchair Soviets"), the columnist Dominic Maurais, also a host on Radio X CHOI, opened his column that day with this incredible salvo:

> It appears the debate over tuition fees has been, for the lunatic fringe,
> nothing but an operetta with an air of class struggle. The Molotov
> cocktails, the trashing of MNA offices, and the bricks on the Metro[1]
> tracks make us look like a banana republic. Our socialist zealots have
> been playing the oppression card as part of a strategy of sabotage. The
> ASSÉ and the CLASSE have stubbornly refused to condemn all violence
> precisely because it is part of their plan. Gabriel Nadeau-Dubois' ASSÉ
> is affiliated with the Union Communiste Libertaire (UCL).[2]

The second largest student federation of Quebec, with one hundred thousand members throughout some sixty cégep and university student associations, representing at that point 70 per cent of striking students, was *in reality*, according to this columnist, a branch of a tiny far-left affinity group that most people had never heard of! Where could Dominic Maurais have gotten such an idea? Could he substantiate his assertions? The rest of his column confirmed what I had already suspected: his allegations were not supported by any proven facts.

Maurais was content to quote the website of the UCL, which stated that some of its members were involved in the movement, in particular through the ASSÉ. Hence, the columnist continued, "the main organs of the ASSÉ and the CLASSE are the UCL blogs *Voix de faits*[3] for the Quebec chapter, and *Cause commune* ["Common cause"], for the Montreal chapter."[4] I was speechless. The argument was pathetic at best. Because the website of an organization says that some of its militants are involved in another organization, the latter is necessarily affiliated with the former? It didn't stand up. And where did he get the idea that the UCL blogs were the "the main organs of the ASSÉ and the CLASSE"? The ASSÉ's website makes it very clear that its newspaper is *L'Ultimatum*. I felt that the reasoning was so poor and the accusation so stupid that this had to be the result of an editorial oversight. I therefore contacted the *Journal de Québec* to let them know.

After waiting a few minutes, I was put through to one of the editors. I calmly explained that one of the columns published that morning contained factual errors, which did not come under the heading of freedom of opinion. That one of their columnists should be opposed to the student strike was quite understandable, but, I went on, as someone in charge of editorial content, he was responsible for ensuring that his newspaper was free of factual errors; the honour of his profession was at stake. I asked him if it would be possible to publish an erratum to apprise readers of the inaccuracies. He uneasily told me that he needed to consult Dominic Maurais and would get back to me.

A few hours later, he called to tell me that the columnist "stood by his opinion" and, consequently, that he would neither withdraw the column nor publish an erratum. "If the columnist is certain of his facts, there's nothing I can do." Yet, as a rule, Quebecor[5] is not unwilling to exert power over its journalists. In fact, article 3.02 of the *Journal de Montréal's* collective agreement unequivocally stipulates that "the employer has and maintains every right to determine the ideological orientation . . . of the company, and to establish its methods of publication." No matter, the article remained online and was shared on social networks by several hundred Internet users. It continued to nurture the hatred and contempt for the students that was Dominic Maurais's stock-in-trade on the radio.

Five months later, the Conseil de presse du Québec (Quebec Press Council) published a decision censuring the columnist, the news editor, and the *Journal de Québec*.[6] The Conseil accepted both grievances of the student who had lodged the complaint, first, for "inaccurate information" and, second, for "defamation." Following its investigation, the Conseil concluded – how could it not? – that Dominic Maurais's allegations were objectively false. Worse than that – and this was something of which the Conseil was unaware – the newspaper maintained those allegations *knowing full well that they were false*, since I had informed the editors of their inaccuracy.

The Conseil de presse du Québec, it should be noted, has no powers of constraint or punishment. Yet this has not made it any more palatable for Quebecor, whose newspapers have withdrawn from the Conseil and refuse to take part in its investigations. Thus, unless we were willing to take the Quebecor empire to court – but who could afford it? – we had no means to oblige it to respect the facts in this case. The mind boggles, because journalism, as we all know, is based on three things: the facts, the facts, and the facts! The moral of the story? In Quebec in 2013, a major newspaper – which, according to the Centre d'études des médias de l'Université Laval (Media studies centre of Université Laval), has a daily circulation of 138,000 copies[7] – can get off scot-free after publishing "inaccurate information" and "defamatory" statements.

If this were just an isolated case, it might be amusing. But anyone who consulted the mainstream media during the spring of 2012 knows that such assertions were commonplace. A veritable collective hysteria took hold of columnists and editorialists, who were suddenly overcome with acute nervous tension that affected their powers of judgment. Defamatory, hateful, and patronizing statements, often completely groundless, proliferated in the public arena. No words seemed hard enough to silence the shouting demonstrators. In the documentary film *Dérives*, Christian Nadeau depicts this phenomenon as an unprecedented wave of *media brutality*. In fact, the media assault did look very much like mental bludgeoning, and the students spontaneously associated it with the kind of bludgeoning practiced by the police. Indeed, the editorial line of the Montreal Police was, to say the least, hard hitting.

The alarmed columnists at first took great pleasure in reducing the demonstrators to a homogeneous group of troublemakers, to which they applied a series of dramatic labels: "hysterical militants," "rebels," "hooligans," "anarchists," "raging vandals," "true savages," "budding terrorists."[8] They then warned their readers not to be fooled by appearances; the student movement was not what it seemed to be, with its nice, colourful demonstrators, its bright young people, its eloquent representatives, and its common-sense demands. In reality, it was infiltrated by "anonymous troublemakers," "delirious ideologues," and "masked and armed goons."[9] Tremble, honourable citizens, the Huns are at the gates of the city! The striking students, assumed to be navel-gazers before the strike, had morphed into dangerous collectivists, "anti-capitalists, revolutionaries, and even anarcho-communists."[10] And the teachers who dared to lend their voices to the strikers' cause were called "semi-retarded," "grubby little profs," and "gangs of parasitic morons."[11]

This amounted to nothing less than denying the *carrés rouges* their status as citizens. So it was not inconsequential that the strikers were consistently alluded to as "overindulged children" (*enfant-rois*) and "rebellious children."[12] We all know how unruly children must be dealt with: they must be put in their place, with a spanking if necessary. Some went even further, casting aspersions on the demonstrators' mental health and the rationality of their approach. Mathieu Bock-Côté noted that "radical anarchism" attracts "problematic personalities,"[13] but it was

Alain Dubuc, in the editorial pages of *La Presse*, who most clearly articulated the negation of the student movement's intelligence:

> This poorly organized movement represents the triumph of passion over reason. Factual arguments, highly unfavourable to the students, were quickly dismissed because the debate shifted onto the territory of emotions. It is hard to engage in discussion with a saucepan! This slide in the debate is easily discernible in the split among the columnists who write opinion pieces for *La Presse*. Those writing in a subjective vein support the student movement, whereas the analytical columnists support the tuition hike. Many people applaud this intrusion of the irrational in the public debate. I don't. Because "the street" can have surprises in store.[14]

Mr. Dubuc felt that the analytical, factual, serious journalists at *La Presse* were all opposed to the students. Apparently he had not read the columns of Michel Girard in *La Presse*'s business section, where he corroborated the students' arguments using quantitative data. Perhaps he was also hasty in his appraisal of the work of Michèle Ouimet, Rima Elkouri, and many other journalists who supported the students to varying degrees. Furthermore, Mr. Dubuc must not have been in touch with the opinion columnists of other newspapers when he surmised that they supported the students. But what is the use of actually reading the people you criticize or of checking your assertions against reality when you are so completely invested with reason?

For commentators like Dubuc, the "student crisis" was neither a major public debate nor a clash of values, but a confrontation between the camp of reason and the camp of madness, between the adults' side and the children's side. They did not criticize the strikers' demands, or their means of action; instead, they rejected the strikers' status as legitimate participants in the public debate ("It is hard to engage in discussion with a saucepan"). Holding a political debate therefore appeared impossible, and negotiations inconceivable. For there can be no possible discussion with a lunatic, and one doesn't negotiate with a capricious child.

This attitude could only provide more ammunition to the Liberal government, whose strategy consisted precisely of not negotiating with the students – of ignoring them – which of course aggravated the crisis and stoked the anger of the protesters. While an informed observer may have wondered at the authorities' refusal to dialogue with those directly affected by the issues on the agenda, the commentators in question preferred to read the situation as a revolt against legitimate authority. They interpreted legitimate opposition to Liberal policies as an assault against democracy and political freedom, no less!

Joseph Facal's nights became haunted by the spectre of the "Kébékistan" revolution, which, in his dreams, would pave the way to the "ACPU, the Anti-Capitalist Planetary Union, originating from the Mercier[15]-Pyongyang-Havana axis," and "little Nadeau-Dubois" could be relied on to supervise the "re-education camps."[16] Such visions may not have raised the level of debate, but they certainly made one shudder. Taking their goosebumps very seriously, the *crème de la crème* of our editorialists rushed to the barricades. The strikers had to be stopped, as their objective was to "defy the government, law, and order, to destabilize society, to take the people hostage, to sap the economy, to undermine the social climate."[17] In his editorial of April 17, André Pratte of *La Presse* warned, "Democracy will give way to anarchy."[18] Two months later, his colleague Dubuc upped the ante: Quebec was drifting dangerously into "a dynamic whereby the street decides," which threatened "the legitimacy of the state, government authority, the decisions of the National Assembly."[19]

The media amplification of social tensions gave rise to an atmosphere of panic, which called for appropriately draconian measures. Law and order had to be maintained; swift action was needed, "otherwise it will be the law of the jungle, might is right. Chaos."[20] Soon after writing this, Benoît Aubin laid it on even thicker in the *Journal de Montréal*, referring to a "conflagration that feeds on itself and is burning out of control, threatening the judicial, political, economic, social, and psychological landscape of Quebec, perhaps even Canada."[21] Isabelle Maréchal, a well-known television and radio journalist, cautioned: "Civil disobedience is not an act of bravery. It is an invitation to disorder and chaos."[22]

Christian Dufour also had his sleep troubled by a "bad dream": "What if the pots and pans never stopped?"[23] A few days later it was the turn of Gilbert Lavoie of *Le Soleil* to succumb to panic, even though he had kept his head throughout the conflict. Now he was having federalist nightmares: "Imagine the passions that could be unleashed in our cities pitting supporters of the 'yes' side against those on the 'no' side in the aftermath of a referendum won by a small margin. It's a nightmare vision that I don't even dare contemplate."[24]

The media hyperbole was such that Éric Duhaime felt compelled to outdo himself. In a show of solicitude, he shared with the public his experience as a target of Islamic terrorism, to remind people that it was possible to "overcome terror." Without a hint of irony, he compared the perils of the Quebec Spring to those of the war in Iraq:

> Having been in the sights of al-Qaeda in Baghdad during the war, it would take a little more from our budding terrorists for me to be intimidated. I learned something in Iraq about how to behave toward those who advocate overthrowing liberal democracy and capitalism: don't change your behaviour in any way. We must not allow ourselves to be terrorized. We must keep our eyes peeled and go on with our lives as usual.[25]

At the height of the pots-and-pans movement, in the days following the mass demonstration of May 22 held in defiance of the special law, what Benoît Aubin feared was a *coup d'état*:

> So here we have an agitated minority, dishing out propaganda while wrapping itself in the flag of rights and freedoms and taking the majority hostage with its actions in order to precipitate a change not so much of government as of the social-economic system, amid a flood of demagogic speeches, violence, intimidation, and disregard for the law and the rights of other citizens, the aim being to destabilize society, bring down the government, and establish a different regime. When democracy is hijacked like this in other countries it's called a putsch. . . . But not here, not if the "good guys" are the ones taking action, even if they cheat, lie, and abuse. . . . Here, it's the Quebec Spring.[26]

A month later, Richard Martineau, always quick to jump to conclusions, wrote "Ce que la crise m'a appris" ("What the crisis taught me"), a sum-up of the strike, two months before it actually ended. And what a terrifying picture he painted, comparing the social climate of the student strike with the climate preceding the major genocides of the twentieth century: "Nothing is more fragile than social peace. For a long time, I wondered how Rwandans and Yugoslavians who had lived in peace with their neighbours for many decades could from one day to the next declare their mutual, murderous hatred and chase one another through the streets brandishing machetes and foaming at the mouth. Now I know."[27] Without Richard Martineau's alertness, Quebec would never have realized that its students were potentially genocidal and that, as a result, it was threatened with unimaginable atrocities.

Now, there is only one possible attitude in the face of a symbolically criminalized enemy: total war. Accordingly, on the eve of the mass demonstration of May 22, Joseph Facal, in his *Journal de Montréal* column, quoted the French philosopher Raymond Aaron, who stated in May 1968: "When student leaders no longer control their troops, when the vandals have taken over, one must choose sides: the state, Parliament, the courts, with all their shortcomings and limitations, or the street and disorder, with its host of harmful side-effects for citizens who did nothing to deserve this." On the day of the demonstration, unwittingly paraphrasing George W. Bush,[28] André Pratte went a step further: "Here is the choice before all the actors in the current crisis: democracy or street violence. It's one or the other."[29] You had to take sides, and the media elite had made its choice. Denying the students their status as legitimate adversaries, it had refused to consider their cause, refused to seriously examine their arguments, turned its back on debate, spit in their faces, shown contempt for their distress, and mocked their hopes. In its eyes, the demonstrators were not even idealists but the "serpent of violence and disorder,"[30] a monster that had to be slain. Whatever it may have claimed, the media elite preferred street fighting to democratic debate. It is understood that the best way to kill someone's dog is to spread the word that it has rabies.

o o o

"Ignore them," I was often advised during the strike. But the problem is precisely that such outrageous comments can't be disregarded. In December 2012, the firm Influence Communication, in its *Bilan de la nouvelle* (Survey of the News), listed the most influential media personalities of the year in terms of speaking time and number of words written. Its conclusions were unassailable: Quebec's public space was very largely dominated by the right.

The legal columnist Claude Poirier topped the list, with an impressive weekly total of seven hours forty minutes and ninety-two thousand words. He put himself in the spotlight with his outburst against the "*carré rouge* delinquents" in mid-May: "Fuck y'all, we don't owe you a thing!"[31] A close runner-up was Mario Dumont, the former MNA for Action démocratique Québec, with six hours fifteen minutes of weekly news commentary. Note that Mr. Dumont's prospects for the coming years are even better, because his number-two ranking did not take into account the column that he started writing for the *Journal de Montréal* at the end of 2012. Rounding out the top three was Richard Martineau (seventy-five thousand words a week), a star columnist of that same newspaper, known for having maintained one of the most negative forums regarding the student strike.

All told, of the fifteen most prominent media personalities, only two came out as relatively sympathetic to the *carrés rouges*: Patrick Lagacé and Marie-France Bazzo. They found themselves in the company of Éric Duhaime, Liza Frulla, Jean Lapierre, Sophie Durocher, René Vézina, and Gilbert Lavoie, all of whom were among the top fifteen and solidly *carrés verts*. The data presented by Influence Communication makes it abundantly clear that the media landscape of Quebec is occupied primarily by commentators located on the right of the political spectrum. It would be wrong to underestimate the impact of this ideological dominance, as the student strike so dramatically demonstrated. How can a democracy be thought of as robust in an environment where the principal forums of public space are monopolized by representatives of a single outlook, especially when they forgo all discernment and in doing so exclude themselves from the debate? How can one hope for a pluralist press if today's journalists are not outraged by the media monopolies? Actually, the average columnist is indeed outraged, but by a fabricated monopoly, a figment, and, straight-faced, he vehemently denounces the fact that "public culture, the dominant culture, that of the media . . . take their cue from the culture of the Left."[32] This comment speaks for itself.

{ Eight }

At the Parthenais Detention Centre

Well, we managed to handcuff him, but in the meantime all the rats that were upstairs . . . the guitar strummers, they're all fucking *carrés rouges* there, all fucking artists of . . . of . . . anyway, shitbags . . .

— Badge No. 728 of the Montreal Police

It was April 27. I was at the Radio-Canada building with my press agent, Renaud Poirier St-Pierre, waiting to be interviewed by Anne-Marie Dussault for the program *24 heures en 60 minutes*. My cellphone rang and Renaud took the call. He froze with a look of surprise on his face. Nodding his head, he said, "Yes, sir, we should be there around eight p.m." Then he turned toward me: "Gab, that was the SQ [the Quebec provincial police]. Apparently you've received some more death threats. This time it's serious. They want to see you this evening at their HQ on Parthenais Street.[1] They're going to offer you protection. We'll go right after the interview." It was by no means the first time I had received death threats. But it was the first time the Sûreté du Québec had contacted us directly, telling us to come right away to their headquarters. And, what's more, to offer me police protection. We did not find this very reassuring.

I dashed over to the SQ headquarters immediately after the interview, along with Renaud and a friend. At the reception desk we were told to wait a few minutes and someone would come for us. Glancing over the shoulder of the officer posted at the reception desk, I noticed something peculiar: all the surveillance cameras in the entrance hall were pointed at me. I moved a few paces to the right. The cameras followed me! When I gingerly shifted to the left, the camera lenses did the same. There were about ten security cameras in the hall, and from what I could see on the monitors they were focused exclusively on my movements. My friends' movements did not interest them in the least. Strange. Why film me like this when they've invited me here to protect me?

At this point, three police arrived. The only one in uniform introduced himself and spoke to my two friends, both of whom dealt with press relations. The officer, who was in charge of communications for the SQ, offered to show them the large press room. "You guys are in comms? You'll see, it's quite something!" Surprised and intrigued, my two companions accepted the invitation and left me alone with the plainclothes police, a man and a woman. They asked me to follow them. We took the elevator up to the tenth floor or so and then walked down a long corridor. A sign caught my eye: *Interrogation Rooms.* Seeing the worried look on my face, the woman reassured me: "Oh, don't worry! These are the only rooms available at this time of day. We're here to talk about your protection, that's all!" I followed the police in good faith, but I was starting to have doubts.

We went into a very small, windowless room furnished with three chairs and a table. I sat down at the table with the policewoman. Behind me, her colleague placed his chair against the door before sitting down. I could no longer leave the room. She began by explaining the reason for the meeting: "Following recent events, with the student crisis growing more and more violent, Minister Dutil[2] asked the Sûreté du Québec to get involved. Not necessarily in the demonstrations, but in terms of intelligence and investigation. So that's the background to our meeting today." Intelligence? Investigation? "I'm Annie B.," she told me, handing me her card, which read: "Annie B., Service des enquêtes sur l'intégrité de la personne, Division des enquêtes sur la menace extrémiste" (Department of investigations on physical threats, Division of investigations on extremist threats). Was I there for my protection or because I represented an "extremist threat"? It was not very clear anymore.

She then spoke about a threatening letter that had been sent to a number of media: an anonymous letter stating that I would be the target of a bomb attack, together with every cégep and university in the province. Of course, they could not accurately assess the seriousness of the threat, but "we don't want to take any chances," she said, and placed a photocopy of the letter on the table. I read the whole thing. It was unremarkable and resembled the ones I was receiving on a daily basis. There was no indication that this one represented more of a danger than the others. The threats and the tone were even somewhat ludicrous (it would take a militia to attack all the cégeps and universities in the province). My doubts started to seem legitimate. Why had they summoned me because of this letter and not the others? Why was I isolated in an interrogation room? Why was the other officer sitting propped up against the door?

The policewoman said she had some questions for me: "In order to adequately protect you, we need to know about your daily life." She asked about my parents, my roommates, my friends, my comings and goings, my habits. I suddenly felt trapped. I was afraid of being locked up for no reason. It wasn't very rational, but under the circumstances such fears seemed to come naturally. The police could very well get everything mixed up – it's been known to happen – and infer that I was "the man behind the scenes" directing the shadowy little groups of "troublemakers" so often mentioned but rarely seen in action.

I remained evasive, providing trivial information that for the most part was already public knowledge. Then the policewoman's questions became increasingly specific, focusing on the CLASSE and my role in it. She appeared to be abreast of the internal tensions in the CLASSE and the student movement more generally, and named Montreal activist groups that might bear a grudge against me. Was she trying to get me to talk about them? I answered that I was not familiar with them, which was true. Gradually, her questions turned into affirmations: "You know that what is happening these days is quite disturbing? You know that you have to be very careful what you say? You know that with the new anti-terrorist laws a person can be accused of provoking fear of a terrorist attack? I'm telling you this for your own good, so you can keep out of trouble." At the time, I was too distressed to realize what she was doing: threatening me.

The interrogation lasted an hour and a half. It ended with this piece of "friendly advice": "If you want to avoid problems, we really need to work together. You have my card. Call me to share any information you may have. For the good of everyone involved." I never called her, nor did I ever hear from her again. When a Radio-Canada journalist personally contacted her a few weeks later, she said she had no recollection of the interrogation. It seems highly unlikely that such a long meeting could be "forgotten," especially since its objective was, theoretically, to protect a student spokesperson who was constantly in the public eye.

On the eve of this mysterious encounter, Robert Dutil made a controversial statement about me: "Mr. Nadeau-Dubois is quite verbose, says all sorts of things, but when we decode his words and put together all his declarations to get an overall picture, what he says amounts to this: all means, including violence, are acceptable in order to get results."[3] This is what he told journalists before repeating the same message on every possible platform throughout the day. According to the police who interrogated me, it had been the minister himself who had asked the SQ to get involved "in the case." Consequently, it is hard not to make the connection between his statement and my being summoned to SQ headquarters the next evening. Soon after the start of the strike, the Liberal strategy was to marginalize the CLASSE so as to weaken its position within the student movement. To this end, its spokesperson needed to be demonized, and the Liberals showed great diligence in trying to accomplish just that. In the eyes of the powers that be, I epitomized social chaos, and, to all appearances, some members of the government had taken a dislike to me. At our first meeting, Line Beauchamp was unable to meet my gaze or speak to me directly; the minister in charge of the law enforcement agencies openly accused me of being a troublemaker; the police went so far as to warn me against myself. All this culminated in the adoption of the special law nullifying the injunctions while stipulating in a specific article that any charges of contempt of court were maintained. But only one such charge had been laid, and it was against me. In fact, Parti Québécois MNA Véronique Hivon dubbed that article the "Nadeau-Dubois clause." One would be hard pressed to find a more telling example of the abuse of institutions and of legislative power for partisan reasons.

The SQ interrogation was simply an exercise in police intimidation. As a spokesperson, I was treated to the "soft" version of police repression, far removed from the truncheons, the pepper spray, and the sound bombs that prevailed in the streets. We have not yet taken the measure of the police violence that was perpetrated in the cities and towns of Quebec during the strike. I am not in the best position to discuss this because my duties as spokesperson prevented me from taking part in most of the street-level actions. But the eyewitness accounts that have been heard since the campaign ended are shocking. This is not a matter of some anecdotes concerning a few isolated incidents, but of a significant institutional dysfunction of police forces.

According to the SPVM (Montreal police service), there were 382 arrests made under the Criminal Code during the student mobilizations in Montreal alone, and 1,711 individuals were taken in for questioning with respect to infractions of municipal bylaws. The data compiled by the Ligue des droits et libertés (Quebec Civil Liberties Union) shows that across Quebec 3,509 individuals were arrested or taken in for questioning, 2,913, or 83 per cent, as a result of kettling. This means that by far the majority of arrests were made indiscriminately, with the police casting their nets to capture shoals of fish and rarely troubling to target only those who had committed an offence. So the vast majority of the arrests were made in violation of two fundamental democratic principles: freedom of expression and freedom of assembly. That some individuals were suspected of breaking the law in no way legitimizes the mass arrest of several hundred people. There was the lamentable episode of May 23, when 518 protesters were kettled and arrested in Montreal, which came after 161 citizens had been detained for hours on April 18 at the Université du Québec en Outaouais for allegedly having infringed an article of the Highway Code. It is beyond dispute that by resorting to mass arrests like these, the police arbitrarily targeted thousands of people solely because they were participating in a demonstration.

Such figures are disturbing, but even more alarming are the tens of thousands of accounts of protesters being personally subjected to police violence, statements that no official inquiry has credited but which the Ligue des droits et libertés endeavoured to compile in a report published in the spring of 2013.[4] Countless people reported being struck, stepped on, slammed to the ground or against a wall, choked, pulled by the hair, dragged along the ground, or repeatedly punched, kneed, or kicked. The results? "Bruises, swelling, sprained wrists, ankles, or necks, and even broken ribs, legs, or arms."[5] On May 1, 2012, a young activist suffered multiple fractures to the skull after attempting to leave a demonstration that had been declared illegal.[6] He is not the only one to have been seriously wounded. Francis Grenier and Maxence Valade will remember the strike for the rest of their lives, having each lost the use of an eye. Permanent loss of hearing, facial bone fractures, concussions – it would take another book to detail the violence committed by the police, particularly the SPVM, during those months of broad-based mobilization. Predictably, the police have denied everything. They have no recollection of any of it, just like the policewoman who interrogated me.

The physical violence of the police occurred by and large amid verbal and psychological violence that beggars description. In the testimonies collected by the Ligue des droits et libertés, there are endless references to insulting, racist, sexist, homophobic, and hateful remarks addressed to students by police on duty. Among the evidence in the report is this statement: "A police grabbed me by the arm. I told him not to touch me or push me, and he replied, 'If I'd have pushed you, you'd have gone flying.' I asked if that was a threat, and he answered aggressively, 'That's a promise.' He drove his bicycle wheel into my groin and told me to move off. I was shaken. I said I was a citizen and that he should treat me with respect, to which he responded, 'you're not a citizen, you're a moron.'"[7] This confirms the findings of a journalist at *La Presse* who interviewed an SPVM employee sympathetic to the students' cause. Here is what he said in answer to the reporter's question about the police's opinion of the demonstrators: "Many see them as overindulged, spoiled children with iPhones, who travel and, what's more, want to have their education paid for."[0] As for the peace officers' feelings toward me personally: "They hate him, intensely," he specified. Apparently, they also gave Martine Desjardins "an unflattering nickname," something "unprintable." So the obscenities proffered by the now famous Badge No. 728 of the SPVM in no way represent an isolated incident, but just the tip of a gigantic iceberg.

Hundreds of demonstrations were held in Quebec in 2012, and nearly all of them were absolutely peaceful. There were very few physical expressions of anger, which is astonishing given the intensity of the crisis and, especially, the contempt and hatred directed at the students. Regarding the symbolic actions and the economic disruptions, such as the occupation of offices, they can be condemned or defended as legitimate tactics, but on the whole they, too, were peaceful. To call them acts of "violence" or "intimidation" amounts to hyperbole verging on demagoguery. From the protesters' perspective, violence and intimidation were manifested primarily in the media and the blows meted out with police batons. For most demonstrators, the skirmishes were provoked by the police, deliberately or otherwise. Did the police break more arms, smash more heads, hit and humiliate more people than the number of broken bank windows? That is a question worth exploring. And by what right can one equate material damages with the brutal aggression perpetrated against citizens by heavily armed police? But leaving aside moral indignation, too often a pretence, what matters is to properly assess the cases of police brutality once and for all. For now, it is the protesters' word against that of the police, and, as it happens, the only ones opposed to an independent inquiry are the police forces.[9]

Throughout the crisis, the police consciously abused the trust that most people in Quebec still place in them – just as they abused my trust when they summoned me on the pretext of protecting me, while their intention was to turn me into an informer or intimidate me. In a democratic society, the population naturally puts its faith in the police. It is morally questionable, to say the least, to exploit that faith in order to deceive the public and justify the unjustifiable. The repression of demonstrations is symptomatic of a dangerous phenomenon: the politicization of the police. It would be a mistake to sweep the danger under the rug by claiming that what happened was nothing more than a few blunders.

{ Nine }

In Defiance

We must carry out acts so utterly bold that even those who repress them will have to admit that an inch of liberation has been won for all.

— Claude Gauvreau

"Monsieur Charest, Sherbrooke. Monsieur Fournier, Saint-Laurent. Madame Courchesne, Fabre." Applause. I can barely see them from where I sit, which is directly overhead. The rules are very strict in the public gallery of the National Assembly: it is forbidden to speak, laugh, or make even the slightest gesture of approval or disapproval. And we are being watched, closely; a few metres to my left, a security guard is staring at us. Actually, this is not very different from watching the debate on television. For the first time in months, I have been confined to the role of spectator. I am literally above the fray. Silent and motionless, I can only watch the action from above.

Minister Courchesne rises with a triumphant smile on her face. She sits down again, but the ovation continues. Her colleagues encircle her, applauding more and more loudly. "Bravo! Bravo!" they shout with forced enthusiasm. She nods her head and looks at them one by one, smiling all the while. The applause stops.

I look up. A heavy silence suddenly pervades the tense atmosphere.

The speaker resumes: "Monsieur Vallières, Richmond. Madame Gagnon-Tremblay, Saint-François. Madame Weil, Notre-Dame-de Grâce. Monsieur Bachang, Outremont." The vote in the first row is over. No matter how far I lean out over the railing, I am unable to see them. But it continues, and shutting one's eyes makes no difference whatsoever. In fact, it seems to be speeding up – "Monsieur Lessard, Frontenac. Madame Thériault, Anjou" – as though someone would like to get it over with post-haste.

As the names roll by in quick succession, a feeling of helplessness wells up inside me. I truly believed that we would be spared the special law. The PQ endeavoured to have the time limit extended so as to defer the parliamentary session until Tuesday, May 22, the day a major march was scheduled to take place. But the Liberals' parliamentary majority is unbeatable. I know now that the adoption of Bill 78 cannot be averted. I wait, and the passivity makes my head spin. In the streets or when I address a crowd or the media, the action relieves my nervousness, but here in the visitors' gallery of the National Assembly I am completely powerless. Stress, anxiety, and anger take hold of me, I am overcome by fatigue, and I have no strength left to listen to the speaker's voice. It has been so long since I had a good night's sleep or took the time to have a proper meal. I am dirty and dead tired. I try to sum things up, to understand how it came to this. Did we make a mistake? I cannot accept that the strike will end on this sour note. Should we have agreed to the initial offer? Should we have been quicker and clearer in condemning violence? Did we go too far? Have the Liberals gone too far?

"Monsieur Pigeon, Charlesbourg." More thunderous applause. They are delighted to restrict civil liberties. This jubilation at the thought of trampling on democratic life doesn't bode well for the student movement. The strike is all well and good, but suddenly it appears quite fragile. I have the impression of seeing it collapse before my eyes. Our stubborn efforts, the assemblies, the debates, the meetings, the laughter and cries of joy, the fury of disagreements, the clash of ideas, all those moments stream through my head as if they were condemned to remain nothing but memories – condemned, in other words, to perish. This vote has to be stopped! I can't reconcile myself to the notion that this act of authority, which is also a sign of Jean Charest's powerlessness, will gag the students. Below the gallery the Liberals are chuckling with satisfaction. They appear to find this breakdown of democracy highly amusing.

The speaker swings around and carries on with the round of voting. I can once again observe the proceedings. "Monsieur Bonnardel, Shefford. Monsieur Rebello, La Prairie." Traitor! At the announcement of the name of François Rebello, former president of the FEUQ (1994–96), the applause swells to new heights: "Bravo! Bravo!" "What conviction!" "A former president of the FEUQ!" The jeers of the Parti Québécois MNAs are surprisingly energetic, considering the long hours they have spent in debate. Apparently the chance of taunting this turncoat has revived them. Their vindictive heckling merges with the noise of the Liberals' desk-thumping machine, a tightly knit phalanx. Beside me, Martine has placed her hands over her face, ashamed of her predecessor. I can't help but smile at the irony of the situation.

The speaker resumes: "Those members opposed to the motion, please rise." "Madame Marois, Charlevoix." The chorus of applause is now even louder than before, but this time it comes from the official opposition. To my eyes, this procedure, where each gesture is calculated, each statement programmed according to the party line, and the protocol and staging all seem unbearably cumbersome. Even the overly long ovation for Pauline Marois rings false, and the bravos too theatrical. Are the Members of the National Assembly merely performers? Do they deliberate to represent us or to put on a show?

Upstanding people – those who need not demonstrate to be heard – maintain that this is the home of Quebec's democracy, however debased it may become, as is currently the case. And yet, barring a few (significant) exceptions, the intellectual calibre of the rhetorical monologues and partisan displays that I observed prior to the vote was simply lamentable. There can be no comparison with the discussion of ideas that I witnessed in the student assemblies before and during the strike. The hollow slogans and phrases that are slung back and forth in the National Assembly, often with scant regard for grammar, pale in contrast to many of the debates among cégep students barely eighteen years old. The National Assembly, which should be a public space, a special place where the public spirit can be expressed, has become a space for publicity, where partisan self-promotion trumps all else. A circus like this has absolutely no grounds to consider itself more honourable than the "street."

"Monsieur Khadir, Mercier. Madame Lapointe, Crémazie. Monsieur Aussant, Nicolet-Yamaska. Monsieur Curzi, Borduas. Are there any abstentions? None? Mr. Secretary-General, the results of the vote, please?"

"Yeas: sixty-eight. Nays: forty-eight. Abstentions: none."

"The motion is thus carried. Consequently, Bill 78, the *Act to enable students to receive instruction from the postsecondary institutions they attend*, has been adopted."

What a vile euphemism that title is! I am beside myself. I have a lump in my throat and my eyes are bloodshot. We fought, imposed a debate that otherwise would never have taken place, but the Liberals have just reminded us that they have the power to ban our movement. The law effectively suspends all academic sessions until August and sets a timetable to make up the winter courses. It strictly forbids anyone from interfering with courses, and, as if that were not enough, it encroaches on the right to demonstrate.

Now that the vote is over, everyone is leaving the Salon bleu.[1] I feel a friendly hand on my shoulder. I vaguely recognize the voice of the CLASSE's press agent: "Time to go, Gabriel. They're waiting." I take a deep breath, then another, and collect myself. Going down the long stairway, I think back to all we did to bring this strike to fruition, only to see it – right now, I am sure of this – snuffed out by this law. In the spacious entrance hall I exchange a few words with Martine, when none other than François Rebello approaches us. He looks at once proud and embarrassed, like a little boy coming to tell to his parents about his part in some prank that went awry. Speaking to my colleague from the FEUQ, he says, "You see? With the amendments that we proposed, the law is a lot better – " Martine cuts him off: "Are you kidding me?" Rebello realizes that there's nothing to be gained and turns on his heels. As I watch him leave I can't help adding, "That's right. Just go away." Certainly not my best rejoinder, but straight from the heart!

We go out for a cigarette while we wait, as planned, for the student federations to finish their press briefings before holding ours. I tell myself that the situation warrants putting aside our differences and addressing the media together. I ask Renaud for his opinion. He thinks it is an excellent idea and immediately makes a few quick calls to see if it might interest the two federations. Meanwhile, I telephone my colleagues on the executive to get their approval. Before too long, Renaud comes over and says, "Forget it, the plan's dead." The FECQ's press agent dismissed the idea out of hand, "because it's out of the question for me to have Léo sitting next to your spokesperson. There's no way I'm going to associate him with you."

A law that threatens the very existence of student associations in Quebec has just been passed. Shouldn't this be the time to close ranks? Their reaction is beyond group self-interest; this is political recklessness, pure and simple. My gut response is to call the FEUQ's vice-president, who has come to Quebec City with Martine. When I inform him of how his colleague at the FECQ replied to our invitation, he lets out a swear word and tells me that he will call her "to sort this out, trust me." In a rage, I answer that I want nothing more to do with the FECQ, that now I'm the one who refuses to hold a press conference with people who treat me like a criminal. Today, in hindsight, I know I should not have reacted that way. I took the affront personally and did not appreciate having the CLASSE snubbed as if it were a marginal faction when, in fact, we represented at the very least three times more strikers than the cégep federation (75,000 compared to 25,000). I lost my self-control. I should have swallowed my pride so that we might speak out against the government with one voice. To indulge one's sensitivity at the expense of solidarity is not very edifying.

While Martine and Léo meet the press, I wait in a narrow corridor and think about what's ahead. I try to foresee how the CLASSE convention, scheduled to begin the next day, will unfold. How will the general assemblies react? Right then, Renaud hands me his cellphone. The home page of the Radio-Canada website shows tens of thousands of protesters marching in Montreal. In defiance of the law! This is the answer to Jean Charest: disobey! I know that I won't be able to say it in so many words when I meet the journalists in a few moments, but I am deeply convinced: opposition to the law is the only option. I look at the pictures of the demonstration and am reassured; when solidarity is needed to stand up to unjust laws, this is always where it can be found. The game is not yet over. Renaud pulls me out of my musings: "Let's go."

∘ ∘ ∘

The process of writing stirs up painful memories. The night the special law was passed, I wept tears of rage. I was certain that the disgust I felt was shared by hundreds of thousands of individuals. When the bill was adopted, the already frail bond of trust between large numbers of Quebecers and democratic institutions finally broke. It is in moments of crisis that a government reveals the stuff it is made of, and Jean Charest's heavy-handedness, which involved suspending fundamental freedoms for the first time since the October Crisis of 1970,[2] laid bare the full extent of his cynicism. To improve its opinion poll ratings and its chances of winning the next elections, this government had just administered electroshocks to Quebec democracy. Jean Charest staked everything on fear, and on the irrational need for security and authority that fear never fails to elicit.

The people's response to the law constituted a mighty antidote to this cynicism. The magnificent and unforeseen pots-and-pans demonstrations that took over the streets each night opened wide the doors of possibility. It was about time. Jean Charest's strategy had reached a breaking point; by polarizing the debate and opting for "law and order," the Liberals had aroused an unparalleled degree of public disgruntlement. The government's entire PR operation – fuelled by the demonization of the carrés rouges – started to founder. Aside from complaining about the noise – as Gérald Tremblay, then mayor of Montreal, did, and he is still the butt of jokes because of it – it was hard to find fault with anything done by the tens of thousands of men, women, and children who, everywhere, every night at the same time, enthusiastically paraded through the streets, so much so that Raymond Bachand publicly described this popular uprising as "good news."[3] This was a radical change of tone coming from someone who only a few days before had declared, "Radical student groups are using intimidation, violence [and] I think it must stop. There are radical groups that consistently want to destabilize Montreal's economy; these are anti-capitalist, Marxist groups. It has nothing to do with tuition fees."[4]

When asked whether the pots-and-pans gatherings were illegal demonstrations, Minister Bachand's bark suddenly became less ferocious. On the pretext that he lacked the legal expertise needed to assess the situation, he answered timidly, "I will not engage in legal interpretations." But not much legal knowledge was required to answer the question. Under the terms of the special law, the pots-and-pans demonstrations were obviously illegal. Indeed, that was their primary raison d'être, and the demonstrators openly asserted this by repeatedly chanting a slogan that was both blasphemous and unifying: "*La loi spéciale, on s'en câlisse* (To hell with the special law)!" That one of the Liberal hawks should be obliged to defer to them attested to the formidable political force of the protest marches. The contempt of the powers that be had encountered a huge obstacle they had not counted on: the people's dignity.

Some time after the special law was adopted, I found myself in a TV studio commenting on the citizens' rallies that since May 19 had been making pots and pans resound throughout Quebec. The person who had preceded me at the microphone was a political columnist for a major Montreal daily who had been asked to analyze the situation. Between our two interviews, during a commercial break, we chatted briefly. He told me that in his neighbourhood there were daily pots-and-pans demonstrations, and his nine-year-old daughter had insisted on participating. Her six-year-old brother, of course, did not want to be left behind, so one day their father gave in and they ended up on the sidewalk with their cookware. The little boy, though overjoyed to be banging on his saucepan, began to wonder what he was doing there, so he asked his big sister. She proudly replied, "The government doesn't want us to demonstrate, so we're demonstratin'!" The columnist added, by way of conclusion, "I don't exactly know what it is, but I have to tell you that you've awakened something very powerful this spring. It will leave its mark on Quebec for good."

The ingenuous answer from the mouth of a little girl speaks volumes about what the pots-and-pans demonstrations represented and the legacy of this movement for Quebec. Not just for the students, but for tens of thousands of Quebecers aged seven to seventy-seven, the spring of 2012 was their first experience of civil disobedience. The little girl expressed in simple terms something that has tended to be forgotten: despite being festive family events, the pots-and-pans demonstrations were held in deliberate defiance of a law adopted by the legislature. That a nine-year-old girl was able to put this so clearly – though obviously without grasping all the implications – illustrates the extent to which civil disobedience permeated society during the student conflict. State authority had to be defied precisely because it had gone beyond what citizens regarded as the acceptable limits of government.

There was something deeply heartening about this spontaneous uprising, which was in part a response to the Liberals' contempt but which also illuminated the strong sense of community and political life abiding in Quebec. It reminded us that, in spite of everything we may have heard, hundreds of thousands of our fellow citizens are still attentive to public issues, concerned about their freedoms, and capable of criticizing those in power. When the pots and pans invaded the streets, many of us breathed a huge sigh of relief: we were not alone, nor were we sheep when we gathered together. The special law and the strict penalties that it prescribed were quite simply rejected by the population. The "street" reduced Jean Charest to silence; civil disobedience was shown to be appropriate at times in a democracy.

This effectively contradicts Jean-Marc Fournier, at that time Liberal minister of justice, who – perhaps still bitter about being defeated by the students in 2005 – declared that "civil disobedience is a nice word for vandalism."[5] For this gentleman, it's an open-and-shut case: civil disobedience is nothing but a refined form of delinquency, a prettified notion that masks widespread contempt for the law and institutions. This opinion was amply broadcast by the usual host of commentators, of whom we will mention only two. Mathieu Bock-Côté, though quite able to go beyond the level of mere opinion, often refers to these events as a rejection of institutions, whereas quite the contrary is true; respect for authority figures should not be confused with respect for institutions. Similarly, four days after the May 22 rally, just when the pots-and-pans demonstrations were at their peak, Denise Bombardier, writing in *Le Devoir* and without a hint of irony, expressed her alarm that the rule of law was on the brink of collapse. In hindsight, her words seem utterly ridiculous: "The street has won out over the rule of law. Laws voted in the National Assembly and enforced by the courts can henceforward be effectively nullified by various groups whose training took place this spring when they bottled up Montreal the Red, took over the social networks, intimidated their opponents, and resorted to violence."[6] It was all over for democracy; Quebec was sinking into chaos. At present, more than two years after the events, many laws have been adopted by the National Assembly and are rigorously applied by the civil service. It must be admitted that Ms. Bombardier had somewhat overstated the threat. On the other hand, the threat represented by the spread of this sort of lack of discernment in the media may be underestimated.

The civil disobedience practiced by the student movement in the wake of Bill 78's adoption was depicted as a slippery slope inevitably leading back to the law of the jungle. To discredit civil disobedience, commentators claimed that it was irreconcilable with democracy because it is supposedly an expression of puerile disregard for the rule of law; this conception is analogous to the one that reduces the protester to an "overindulged child," resistant to sacrifice and authority. Nothing could be further from the truth. Civil disobedience does not mean rejecting all laws at all times for any reason whatsoever. Those who lecture the student movement and the citizens who supported it forget that people respect laws not simply because of their *official* status as law, and even less out of a primitive fear of being punished. What is also at work, and on a far deeper level, is their adherence to the principles and values underpinning the law, of which specific laws ought to be the positive manifestations. Thus, what prompts the vast majority of workers to pay taxes is not merely fear of the Revenue Agency; it is also, and especially, their awareness that it is necessary and desirable to pool certain resources in order to ensure the provision of basic public services. To a large degree, laws are observed because they are felt to be just. When they or the powers that enact them fail to have their legitimacy recognized, they are liable to engender resistance.

It is often tempting to view the police baton as a symbol of the strength of the state, but it is, on the contrary, proof of its weakness. Initially, Law 78 appeared to be a show of strength and a sign of authoritarianism. In reality, however, it demonstrated the exhaustion and despair of a government backed into a corner. It was its inability to solve the crisis through ordinary political means that forced Jean Charest's Liberal government to resort to extraordinary legislative means. In so doing, it crossed a line and betrayed the fundamental principles on which our political order, *theoretically*, is based – that is, freedom of expression, conscience, and association. It was in reaction to this dangerous drift that the pots and pans rang out, as if to say, "Enough! You've gone too far." The hundreds of thousands of Quebecers who marched in the streets each night were not expressing a simple-minded rejection of political authority and institutions. Instead, they were putting forward a very straightforward demand: that political authority and institutions live up to the principles on which they are grounded, to serve the common good and not the interests of its administrators. If the pots-and-pans demonstrations were illegal, it was not because the families that took part in them were hostile to the rule of law, but rather because the state itself, charged with defending the rule of law, had gone astray in adopting a law that violated the fundamental principles of our society. Hence the pride and emotion evinced by those protests. While delinquency occurs in the margin and in the shadows, the pots and pans resounded in broad daylight for everyone to see and hear. What made this action stand out was its public nature.

Expressing neither simplistic contempt for the rule of law, nor child-ish obstinacy in the search for privilege, the pots and pans were, rather, the affirmation of an important principle, which Pierre Vadeboncoeur[7] has called the people's authority. In brandishing their pots and pans, the people showed that they are always sovereign, or, at any rate, that they quickly become sovereign when the occasion arises. Civil disobedience is not a mere refusal to obey; what it contests is not the existence of laws, but the transgressions of those who enact them. It does not reject insti-tutions, but their abuse. In this sense, civil disobedience is profoundly democratic.

There were times when I was uncomfortable with some of the posi-tions that I had to defend in my capacity as spokesperson for the CLASSE, but no press conference has made me feel prouder than the one I gave on May 21 at Émilie-Gamelin square.[8] While the two student fed-erations and the trade-union organizations were timidly announcing that they would respect the special law, the coalition that I, together with Jeanne Reynolds, represented displayed dignity and courage by making known its intention to pursue the mobilization regardless of the special law. This was not, however, a gratuitous posture of defiance; that day, we simply declared that we would continue to mobilize as we had always done by virtue of the freedoms guaranteed in various charters, without modifying our practices on the basis of Law 78. This was the moment when the CLASSE demonstrated that it had gone beyond the status of student association. We were an organization participating in a citizens' movement.

What happened next is well known. Through large-scale disobedi-ence, the population of Quebec made Law 78 inapplicable, except for the suspension of courses. Long before the government of Pauline Marois formally abolished it in September 2012, the citizens had already done so through their mobilization: no notices of infraction, no fines, and no arrests were made under Law 78. In spite of the press conference where it openly declared its intention to break the law, in spite of having orga-nized an illegal demonstration 250,000 strong on May 22, the CLASSE was never fined a single dollar, nor even contacted by an investigator.

What we witnessed was not just civil disobedience on an unprecedented scale but a momentous victory of this form of protest.

In a defiant speech addressed to Judge Ouimet during the famous *procès des Cinq* (trial of the Five) in 1971,[9] Michel Chartrand quoted Pierre Elliott Trudeau: "It is the duty of citizens to examine their conscience as to the quality of the social order by which they are bound and of the political authority that they accept. . . . No government nor any regime has the absolute right to exist." This should give pause to those who were offended at the sight of hundreds of thousands of Quebecers disobeying a law that was denounced by the Barreau du Québec (the Quebec Bar), Amnesty International, the Commission des droits de la personne et de la jeunesse du Québec (Quebec commission for human rights and the rights of children and youths), and a UN observer. Rather, it is the young people of Quebec who should be worried about the leadership of a political and media elite whose conception of society and institutions is impoverished to the point where it sees society as merely a collection of individuals, and institutions as hollow shells that must be meekly obeyed in all circumstances. Looking ahead, there is cause for celebration inasmuch as the generation that will take charge of the land in a few years has already had the courage to stand in defiance of leaders who, having been left to their own devices, have forgotten the constituency they are supposed to serve.

{ Ten }

Under the Shield of the Law

There is no greater tyranny than that which is perpetrated under the shield of the law.
— attributed to Montesquieu

Two months almost to the day after the start of the strike, Jean-François Morasse, a fine arts student at Université Laval, was granted an injunction by the Quebec Superior Court guaranteeing him full access to his courses. Despite the strike mandate obtained through a democratic vote and the fact that the professors in his department were abiding by the mandate, Mr. Morasse insisted on attending his courses. "It is incomprehensible that people can be made to suffer this much in the name of a social cause. I can't get my head around it," he complained to a Radio-Canada journalist.[1] Moreover, Morasse frankly admitted that he had not attended the general assembly where the strike mandate was adopted because he had not felt concerned. In retrospect, it may be tempting to grant him this point, for what is the use of participating in democratic deliberations if one can afterwards circumvent them by appealing to the courts? The court order he obtained would be one of the few to be respected during the strike. Student Morasse gained full access to his courses and completed them on time. But this was not enough for him. Two months later he laid charges of contempt of court against me, alleging that a statement I had made on

RDI was an incitement to flout the injunction handed down by the Superior Court. Jean-François Morasse, whom a lawyer and a lawsuit had transformed into a courageous champion of the law fighting the infamous strike in the face of all opposition, went so far as to publicly call for my imprisonment. The attempt to break the strike by resorting to the courts opened a new chapter in the history of the strike. But the script remained essentially unchanged.

Before the courts, the plaintiffs seeking injunctions pleaded what all opponents to the strike demanded, a proposition made popular by Arielle Grenier during her memorable appearance on the set of the popular talk show *Tout le monde en parle*: that is, the inalienable private right of students to attend the courses they had paid for. They were asking the courts to enforce that purchase agreement. This was not the first time in legal history that private rights were trotted out to contest the legitimacy of the right to association and, more broadly, social rights. In the early twentieth century, many social laws were similarly attacked by the courts. A narrowly liberal mind will find it perfectly natural to protect individual freedoms, property, and contracts against the tyranny of the majority and the abuses of collective power. Conversely, it is self-evident that a democrat will demand the same protection for collective political aims and rights against individual whims and arbitrariness; corruption, abuse of power, and tyranny are terms for the unilateral subordination of institutions to such interests. The judges quickly concluded that in this conflict, individual, contractual rights overrode collective rights of a political nature. This approach led them to spurn the political essence of the strike and thus to commit a serious error in their assessment of the facts.

Political reality demands that one belong to a group and submit, on occasion, to group decisions. It is called living in society, and humans are still, by all accounts, social animals. This notion was beyond the grasp of Laurent Proulx, a law student and former soldier, who justified the injunctions by denouncing the "solidarity of force" advocated by the student movement. How many times have I heard these arguments: "Some have the right to be for the tuition hike, while others have the right to be against it"; "Those who want to can strike, while the others can attend their courses"? Everyone for him or herself, and all agreeing on one thing: to share nothing and to leave each other alone. Of course, no one would dare frame the agenda in such crude terms, and great care is taken to disguise such egoism as a generous openness to others. Writing in the online journal *Le Prince Arthur*, Laurent Proulx described at length the thinking that had led him to ask for an injunction: "In my heart of hearts I was genuinely convinced that preventing access to classrooms was illegal. Understand me: three years ago I fought in Afghanistan to ensure free access to schools for Afghan women and children."[2] In his own way, he was fighting for access to education!

The strike was not brought on by a private dispute. It was a social crisis with political stakes: the direction post-secondary education would take in Quebec. The right to education, whether Laurent Proulx likes it or not, makes the state responsible for providing its population with a high-quality, free, and accessible education system, but it in no way obliges society to honour the agreement that Université Laval signed with Laurent Proulx. Private contracts are fragile arrangements that can easily be reneged on, as Laurent Proulx himself demonstrated by dropping the course that was the object of the injunction he had requested. But one cannot so casually back out of a social contract; when it is broken, when institutions are allowed to fall apart, whole groups – not just individuals – are affected.

The injunctions to allow access to courses during the strike were granted on the grounds that paying tuition fees confers on a student the right to demand the desired instruction. On the basis of this principle, the courts had to reduce the scope of students' right to association and, especially, refuse to acknowledge the existence of the strike. Judge Gaétan Dumais, on issuing an injunction for the Université de Sherbrooke, drew this astonishing comparison:

> The movement to boycott courses organized by the student associations is akin to any boycott that might be organized against a grape juice producer or a department store. A person cannot be obliged to do or prevented from doing business with a grape juice producer or a

department store. This is an individual choice. If a group decides to organize a boycott of any company whatsoever, it can do so. However, when a person decides to boycott a company, he may not prevent access to that company. The same holds true in the case of universities.[3]

A short time later, this grape-juice lover reproduced this edifying analogy word for word in the formulation of his injunction for the Cégep de Sherbrooke.

When it voted in the law on the accreditation and funding of student associations, which allows student unions to be constituted on the model of the Rand formula (automatic check-off), the Quebec parliament chose to encourage students to unite to defend their rights. From a strictly legal perspective, freedom of association entails the freedom of political expression, the possibility of negotiating agreements, and the right to strike. The law governing student associations does not, however, mention the right to strike. Hence, there are jurists who deny its existence, and others who defend the exercise of this right. Based on the fact that the law on student associations does not explicitly mention the right to strike, the magistrates almost unanimously issued injunctions to put an end to the walkouts. But if one refers to case law, the history of Quebec leaves no room for doubt: for over forty years, student strikes have been so frequent that they have been in a way culturally institutionalized.

The notion of "boycotting" courses is nothing but a Liberal rhetorical invention. It is an uncommon term in the political history of modern Quebec. The Liberals themselves – including Jean Charest – recognized that the 2005 mobilization around the loan and bursary system was indeed a "strike." In 1996, the PQ as well had referred to a "student strike." Actually, ever since the 1960s, students' right to strike has become customary in Quebec and has been tacitly recognized by college and university administrations, as well as by every provincial government. Jean Charest, in his 1998 biography, uses the term "strike" when he harks back to his youth as a student: "I must admit that I did not study much that year. I was more interested in the affairs of the student council. There were 1,200 students in the school. We organized strikes, protests, and negotiations with the teachers."[4] What's more, on February 14, 2012, the day the CLASSE launched the strike, Line Beauchamp publicly referred to the "right to strike": "There are 11,000 students who have decided to exercise their right to *strike*, out of a total of 475,000 university and cégep students, that is, a little over 2% of students are on *strike*."[5]

The Liberal government waited until the strike was several weeks old before suddenly deciding to redefine the movement as a "boycott," probably on the advice of the public relations firm hired to manage the crisis. This paved the way for the injunction requests that, predictably, were submitted a few weeks later. Would a wholesale recourse such as this have been possible in 2005, when all the actors publicly acknowledged that there was indeed a "strike" going on? I seriously doubt it. In sum, a political decision had triggered the conflict, and now it was once again an element of political discourse that served to push the conflict into the ambit of the courts.

Unfortunately, the ideas that ought to inform political discussion tend to dissolve in procedural wrangling. The debate that should have been conducted on the main choices confronting society was atrophied to the point where it became nothing more than the case of *Jean-François Morasse v. Gabriel Nadeau-Dubois*. So much energy was expended to avoid debating with the students! So much effort was put into denying the relevance of our ideas and even the very existence of our movement! In this unsavoury circus, there were many who outdid themselves and each other to bury the social issues in legal proceedings.

In an article published in *Le Devoir*, Christian Brunelle, a law professor at Université Laval, pointed out that an injunction must order a party to "accomplish a specific act or operation," and that "it must be enforceable."[6] Yet, as noted by this legal expert, many of the injunctions in question stipulated that instruction must be provided in a "normal way," which, given the context of the crisis, was completely unrealistic. Unless, of course, one deemed it normal to have a course given to a single student ... surrounded by a clutch of journalists and a police squad! In actual fact, the injunctions shifted the government's responsibilities onto the backs of the cégeps and universities while at the same time pouring oil on the fire. Still worse, according to Brunelle, was that by deliberately obscuring the collective dimension of the conflict, the judges ran the risk of weakening the authority of the courts and jeopardized "the primacy of the law."

On only a few rare occasions did the students obey the judges' rulings. It was a predictable response. One would have to be rather naive to believe that after weeks of marching in the streets, the strikers would quietly go back home, that they would meekly comply with a court order requested by those – their classmates among them – who had lost the debates in the general assemblies. In the universities and cégeps, the students were quick to understand that the outcome of the strike depended on that of the injunctions. To comply would have meant the end of their struggle; if courses were given to one or two students, every striker would have to personally assume the academic consequences of her or his absence. Without the assurance that came from the recognition (voluntary or not) of the strike by the academic administrations, student solidarity was in danger of fracturing, especially after more than ten weeks on strike. We had to hold the line at all costs – this was the opinion of students on every campus, regardless of which among the FEUQ, the FECQ, or the ASSÉ represented them.

The CLASSE – least of all Jeanne or I – never called for the injunctions to be breached. The striking students did so naturally, almost as a reflex. On some of the campuses affiliated with student federations, the association presidents put out calls to respect the courts' decision, to no avail. At Collège Rosemont, Léo Bureau-Blouin even put in a personal appearance, holding a bullhorn, to ask students and their supporters to take down the picket line – in sum, to let the strikebreakers beat them. This earned him some words of congratulation from Judge Denis Jacques when he convicted me of contempt of court.[7] In sum, the only effect of Léo's appeal, made in spectacular fashion before the TV cameras, was to please the judges.

As for me, I had decided to stick to defending the legitimacy of the strike mandates. Here is the position that I expressed on air at Radio-

Canada and for which I was subsequently accused of being in contempt of court:

> Clearly, these decisions, these attempts to force a return to the class-rooms, never work because the students who have been on strike for thirteen weeks are all united ... they respect the democratic mandate that was determined through the strike vote, and I think it is altogether legitimate for students to take measures to apply the democratic choice that was made to go on strike. It is very unfortunate that what is truly a minority of students is using the courts to circumvent a collective decision. So we believe it is perfectly legitimate for people to do what is necessary for the strike vote to be respected, and if it takes picket lines then we think this is an entirely legitimate means.

In spite of the legal consequences and complications stemming from this statement, I do not regret a single word. While some chose to adopt a calculated, strategic discourse, I preferred to defend my convictions and disregard the fear that was the intended effect of judicializing the political conflict. Even now, I am convinced that my words conveyed a valid opinion, a needed criticism of the widespread recourse to injunctions, and a defence of the right to strike, all of which are acceptable in any society claiming to be democratic. The columnist Yves Boisvert observed, "If the criteria of the penal code were applied rather than those of prevailing morality," there would be reasonable grounds to doubt that I had acted in contempt of court.[8] According to Boisvert, there is "no legal obligation to be a good boy like Léo Bureau-Blouin."

Given such a long and polarized political dispute, how could the judges believe for even a moment that their ordinances would actually be put into effect? For many striking students, the widespread recourse to injunctions constituted a political abuse of the courts, especially because they recognized in the injunctions the arguments and the vision of public institutions that the strikers were fighting day in, day out on their campuses and in the public arena. Overall, it is regrettable that the presiding judges did not assess the degree of political tension underlying the applications for injunctions. Yet it was not the first time the Quebec judiciary was confronted with this sort of dilemma.

At the Montreal law courts on February 4, 1971, in defending himself against the accusation of "seditious conspiracy" made in the wake of the events of October 1970, Michel Chartrand cautioned Judge Ouimet about the pernicious effects of using the courts for political purposes. His address, delivered admittedly in far more dramatic circumstances than ours, is nonetheless worth quoting:

> Your Honour, justice is not something that can be toyed with for very long. Young people are impatient. They will not endure it for as long as their fathers did, whether we like it or not. They have shed their ignorance complex. They are aware of what is happening. They are able to distinguish between courts that carry out justice and courts that engender injustice. However, if they realize as well that nothing is being done to keep the courts that engender injustice from deteriorating, well then, they will lump together all the courts.[9]

There are numerous precedents to be found deep in the judicial archives showing the limitations of injunctions in situations of social conflict. In the mid-1970s, to take just one example, Judge Jules Deschênes, in a moment of clear-sightedness, refused to condemn the bus drivers of the Société de transports de Montréal (Montreal public transit corporation) a second time for contempt of court. "Will we be obliged to erect special facilities for these 1,600 prisoners and, more importantly, do we think this draconian measure will get the Metro and the buses running again?" he asked, going so far as to describe the employer's demands as "socially, politically, and legally inappropriate in their conception and dangerous in their consequences." Judge Duschênes went still further, flatly refusing to interfere with a political conflict that was rapidly worsening: "Until the political authorities find the remedies needed to resolve these social conflicts, I am of the opinion that the Superior Court must not lend its authority to the subjugation of a mass of citizens through fines and imprisonment . . . [nor] must it take part in an act that is bound to fail and is unsuited to resolving a social crisis that, for some time now, has been in the purview of the political authorities."[10] This judgment ought to be high on the reading list of the current judiciary. A social crisis calls for a negotiated, political solution. The government of Jean Charest was ultimately obliged to face reality – though, as always, in its own offhand way – by adopting a special law in May that nullified all the injunctions, thereby acknowledging that no realistic resolution of the crisis could be expected from allowing them to accumulate.

When I received the ruling on my trial a number of weeks later,[11] I was taken aback – and I was not alone in this – by the intransigence of its tone. Judge Jacques couched his verdict in stern language, quoting none other than John F. Kennedy:

> Our nation rests on the principle that observance of the law is the eternal rampart of freedom, and that defiance of the law is the surest road to tyranny. Citizens are free to disagree with the law but not to disobey it. For in a government ruled by laws and not by men, no citizen, regardless of his power or the importance of his position, nor any group, however rebellious and undisciplined it may be, has the right to defy a court of justice.

The judge also took the liberty of comparing me to my opposite number in the FECQ, Léo Bureau-Blouin, emphasizing that his appeal for the injunctions to be respected contrasted with my position, which "advocates, instead, anarchy, and encourages civil disobedience." Anarchy, no less! One is entitled to ask how in the world Judge Jacques came up with this assertion, since neither the evidence submitted to him nor the statements made by Jean-François Morasse's lawyer contained any such allegations.

My sentence came down a month later: 120 hours of community service. In his second judgment,[12] Judge Jacques continued from where he had left off. He referred to the "deeply ingrained mindset" displayed in my general call to disobey the injunctions in order to ensure compliance with a "so-called strike vote." He added that I had "not even tried to explain or to qualify those statements," as if my exercising the right to remain silent and not testify at the trial proved my guilt. Moreover, the judge deplored "the unjustified attacks and the threats" made against Jean-François Morasse, while saying nothing about those that I had been subjected to. Yet it was public knowledge – and we pointed this out to the court – that I had received countless explicit threats throughout the strike, both in private and in broad daylight, including, for instance, those proffered over the airwaves of the trash radio stations in Quebec City.

The two judgments rendered by Judge Denis Jacques in my case were, to say the least, unusual in both tone and approach. In this instance, as in many others, the magistrate based his rationale on a binary opposition, symptomatic of a rigid interpretation of the law, between absolute, blind obedience to laws and social chaos.

Some twenty days before the first hearing in my trial, the chief justice of the Quebec Superior Court, François Rolland, in keeping with tradition, gave a speech to launch the new judicial session, also known as the *ouverture des tribunaux* (opening of the courts).[13] Chief Justice Rolland had taken charge of the great majority of the applications for interlocutory injunctions submitted during the strike, and his court was faced with a major problem of consistency, with some judges granting injunctions and others not. For the legal profession, this address, delivered each year to a large number of lawyers and judges from various Quebec courts, has a good deal of symbolic significance. In it, the chief justice presents his vision of the issues currently facing jurists throughout the province.

The theme of the speech should come as no surprise: "Majority, democracy, and the primacy of law."[14] As might be expected, Judge Rolland offered a lengthy exposition – I will not recapitulate it here – whose thrust was to remind the judiciary that "respect for the Constitution and the primacy of law are the basis of our system of government," that "the primacy of law implies, first, that the law is above the citizen," that there is "only one law for all. And all are subject to the laws."[15] He quoted in turn judges, constitutionalists, and philosophers to prove that the primacy of law is synonymous with public order and that the aim of this principle is to provide "citizens and residents with a stable, predictable, and orderly society in which to conduct their activities."[16] He noted that the role of lawyers and judges is to defend this system and explain it to the population, because if the officers of justice do not adhere to this principle, "our democratic workings as a whole are undermined."[17] Moreover, the Honourable François Rolland described the role of the courts as that of ensuring the maintenance of security and social peace. Should this be read as an allusion to the protests that many jurists voiced against Bill 78, which its supporters defended as necessary precisely in order to bring back social peace?

But the most memorable part of Judge Rolland's oration was no doubt the conclusion:

> When we take things for granted, we sometimes forget how important they are. Consider oxygen: we realize its importance when it is lacking. The student conflict unfolding in Quebec since last winter and its excesses demonstrate the fragility of the democratic system and its vulnerability. It is certainly comforting to live in a free and democratic society, but we must be conscious of it. This freedom is part of our daily lives, but we must remember that it was won at a high cost. I would like every one of us to always be mindful of the priceless legacy that has been bequeathed to us, so that we, in turn, may do likewise for the generations to come.[18]

With this final statement, the chief justice of the Superior Court endorsed the viewpoint of right-wing columnists. From the heights of his status as chief justice, he essentially declared that the student conflict constituted a threat to freedom and democracy. By what strange acrobatic leap did a judge come to regard as a serious threat to democracy a peaceful civil disobedience movement protesting a law that had been denounced by the Quebec Human Rights Commission, the UN High Commissioner for Human Rights, Amnesty International, and the Barreau du Québec (Quebec Bar Association) precisely because it represented an excessive restriction of the fundamental freedoms underpinning our society? Throughout his speech, Judge Rolland placed himself above the population, and adopted a not-very-reassuring attitude: "We have an important role to play, we lawyers and judges and other agents of justice, especially because we are, in a way by virtue of our positions, trustees and guardians. And we must explain this system to the citizens so that they may understand it."[19]

As for me, it was the content of this speech that, more than anything else, gave me reason to worry about the state of our democracy. It indicated that some judges – there are of course many notable exceptions – uphold a, to say the least, narrow conception of democracy, which they too often associate with their own decisions. Are some individuals more citizens than others, supposedly by virtue of their mission to teach people the true nature of democracy? This brings to mind the attitude of other actors in this conflict, who put forward their political position as the only rational and legitimate option.

There is cause to be alarmed here – far more, in any case, than by a gathering of middle-class citizens banging on saucepans with wooden spoons, even when they are chanting their utter disdain for a law.

Postscript

In January 2015, the Quebec Court of Appeal unanimously overturned the decision of the Superior Court. More than two years after the end of the student strike, I was acquitted of the charges of contempt. The Court of Appeal rejected the claims of the plaintiff, Jean-François Morasse, in harsh terms and reprimanded Justice Denis Jacques for having accepted his lawyer's arguments. The Court of Appeal found that the lower court judge had incorrectly assessed the evidence and, furthermore, had made an "unreasonable extrapolation" by accusing me of advocating "anarchy" and "civil disobedience." Immediately applauded by observers of the legal scene, the ruling was unequivocal: my statement of May 13, 2012, had in no way constituted contempt of court. Today, I feel that justice has been done and that the legal system has finally treated me with respect.

Less than forty-eight hours after my acquittal was made known, Morasse announced that he would take the case to the Supreme Court of

Canada. The next day, he received official support from two Quebec City radio hosts – Éric Duhaime and Nathalie Normandeau – who called on the public to assist him financially. Duhaime is a controversial, openly libertarian commentator, and Normandeau, a former Liberal minister in the Charest government, is under strong suspicions of corruption. They also plan to hold a funding event to encourage the plaintiff and have each pledged the symbolic sum of one hundred dollars. At the same time, Morasse has proudly declared his intention to run in the fall 2015 federal election under the Conservative banner.

As of this writing, there is no way of knowing whether the Supreme Court will agree to hear the case, but many political analysts have said they would be surprised if it does. However that may be, I have the unpleasant feeling of being the object of a wider political strategy. Apparently, there are some who believe in the benefits of nourishing a certain image of the events of 2012. Having the procedures drag on enables them to keep on representing the student strike as a troublesome time of social disruption and contempt for democratic institutions.

Clearly, the struggle for the representation of the Quebec students' spring is far from over.

{ Eleven }

All for What?

Au revoir adieu!
When we return
we'll have the past at our backs
And by dint of hatred for
all servitudes
We shall be the savage beasts of hope.
— Gaston Miron

Victory? Defeat? Tie game? The citizens who mobilized in the spring of 2012 persist in posing the question: What has come of all their efforts? People still ask me this in the street. What if we did it all for nothing? These are legitimate questions. A year after the strike, one gets the unpleasant impression that little has changed in Quebec. The elections called by Jean Charest, which apparently succeeded in putting a lid on the situation, did not generate any great hopes. Many people emerged from the strike scarred and haunted by the feeling that it had been no more than a sunny break in otherwise dark times. Was the spring just a blip? The revolt of a small, strident fringe group? A veteran trade-unionist once told me, "Political struggle is not a game of hockey. There's no siren going off so you can tell yourself, 'Okay, it's over, we've won!' No, it's never clear-cut. You always have to start over, but that's how you move forward." Social battles, especially the very long ones, rarely end with victories, and our strike was no exception to that rule.

For months, the Liberals continued to crank up the repression with the aim of halting the mobilization, of breaking the opposition – that's how energetic the movement was. In the end, they were left holding just one card, and by playing it they very nearly walked away with the winnings. In August 2012, Jean Charest called a general election. This was a first for the student movement. We had felled a government, or, at the very least, played a major part in ousting it. But there was the risk of seeing victory turn into a trap, should the strike enable Jean Charest to return to power.

Owing to the launch of the elections – the Liberals must have guessed this – the strife within the CLASSE reached new heights. Even now, the very mention of those debates is enough to spark the anger of many activists who were involved in the student movement at the time. The coalition's convention found itself in an awkward position. Most of the strike mandates were several months old, and summer is not a good time to bring students together. In addition, we were well aware that electoral debates have always been divisive for the most militant student unions. Given the impossibility of consulting the general assemblies, the convention adopted a rather wimpish position: no watchword would be issued concerning the pursuit of the strike, and the coalition would stay neutral on the issue of "election choices." This meant two things. First, the CLASSE would not call for either the continuation or the end of the strike at the general assemblies scheduled for early August. Second, the CLASSE would not provide its members with guidance on the elections: there would be no call to either vote or abstain, let alone to vote for or against a particular party. For the organization, this position had the advantage of avoiding the need to decide a debate that would have led to the coalition's disintegration. But it turned out to be ill advised in the public arena. No one really knew what the CLASSE wanted, not even its own members – naturally, since the CLASSE convention had decided not to take a position, at least not initially. At the following convention the CLASSE was obliged to take a different tack, and recommended pursuing the strike despite the elections. The students' general assemblies, meanwhile, were far less ambivalent once they had the opportunity to express themselves. Without wavering, they voted almost unanimously to go back to school.

It was against this backdrop that I decided in early August 2012 to tender my resignation as spokesperson for the CLASSE. To publicly defend the continuation of the strike in spite of the elections, knowing full well that the assemblies had not been consulted for months – it all made me feel extremely uncomfortable. There had always been a slight gap between my personal positions and those of the organization that I represented. This was normal and even healthy, as I was a spokesperson and not a leader. This time, however, the gap was too wide. It was time for me to leave. Also, the fatigue had been building up for months, and I felt I was being used by the Liberals, as everyone expected Jean Charest to raise the spectre of the *carrés rouges* and of "Gabriel Nadeau-Dubois" to win the elections. I could not reconcile myself to playing that role.

What followed is well known. The Liberals were defeated and the Péquistes[1] came to power by the skin of their teeth. The tuition fee increases and the special law were quickly abrogated. The two main demands of the strike movement were met. But this did not suffice to end the debates. A significant portion of the coalition's most militant core, where the strike had kindled the hope of more profound social change, still hesitates – in a way, justifiably – to call the strike a victory. Knowing, however, that the Liberals were determined to never yield to the student movement, we could not reasonably have hoped for a better outcome. Over the short term, what more could we have achieved than the cancellation of the tuition hike and the ejection of the Liberals? The indexation of tuition fees, the Marois government's alternative solution, rests on the same ideological foundations as the Liberals' increase but does not have the same effect on access to education, even in the long run, because the Liberals' plan included the indexation of tuition fees as of 2017, the final year of the five-year increase of $1,625. The student strike thus allowed thousands of young Quebecers to go to university. While the citizens' movement put forward broader demands, it should be borne in mind that the tuition hike was at the root of the mobilization. And it was abolished. This may not have been El Dorado, but it was no trifle, either.

There was cause for disappointment on another level. The PQ government that replaced that of Jean Charest did not alter the basic direction of Quebec society, nor was there anything to suggest that it would do so anytime soon. The perennial "deficit zero" objective continued to reign supreme among government priorities, to the detriment of funding for and better access to public services. The feeble tax reforms promised by the PQ were soon abandoned or diluted in response to the business community's complaints, which did not require a strike to be heard. A slight grimace, a little "tax anxiety," and a few press releases were enough to make the government retreat. The picture is hardly prettier when it comes to the environment. The moratorium on shale gas exploration was heartening, the mining bill had one or two teeth, but otherwise it was business as usual. It truly felt as if we had gone back to square one.

This was not the first time that mass mobilizations produced meagre short-term results. To cite just one example, in 1972 the *front commun syndical*, the united front of union organizations, and the broad-based reaction to its leaders' imprisonment did not disrupt the established order.[2] On the contrary, even though the union movement won the strike's main demand, in October 1973 the Liberal Party, led by Robert Bourassa, secured the largest parliamentary majority in the history of Quebec, with 102 seats out of 110. One can only imagine the disappointment of those hoping for a change of government, especially in light of the fact that the mobilization of 1972 had been preceded by the ferment of October 1970. But history had not had its last say. Three years after Bourassa's spectacular triumph, René Lévesque's young PQ was voted into power. It took a number of years for the rank-and-file mobilization of social movements to bring about a major electoral overhaul.

Still, the disappointments and open wounds of the strike cannot be reduced to election issues. When political passion of this intensity subsides, it leaves a vacuum in its wake. The reasons to fret and to fight, starting with the ecological disaster produced by the dynamics of capitalism, are just as numerous today. Yet the streets are quiet. Should we despair? I am not so sure. That the fruits of the spring were not harvested the very next fall is no cause for alarm. On closer examination, one sees that the hundreds of thousands of people who mobilized in 2012 are active within society on a daily basis; young and old alike have renewed their interest in public affairs and now understand social involvement in concrete terms. With a little luck, these people will remain committed. Ours is a small society, and the many thousands who demonstrated in Montreal during the spring of 2012, not to mention all those who supported the movement without being able to march in the streets, will necessarily have an impact on society as a whole. The student strike showed us that there are still people in Quebec who continue to hold to another conception of the land and of themselves. There are students who aspire to something more than a large income, teachers who care about culture, workers who still have a sense of work well done and of service to the community, scientists who still want to understand what life is, musicians and artists who are reinventing our culture, and activists who defend the solidarities that make Quebec what it is.

A few more years will still be needed before the results of what started in the spring of 2012 become visible. This is frustrating, no doubt, but haste is not an argument. Societies change gradually, and even major upheavals are always the result of the workings of history over time. Political commitment demands patience. It's a marathon, not a sprint. The veteran poet and songwriter Gilles Vigneault[3] once explained this to me in his own way: "When I started performing, people in the audience were very quiet. These days they sing, whistle, shout, applaud. People want to be part of the show, Gabriel. This doesn't always make life easy for the singer, but it's a wonderful asset for Quebec: more and more, they're demonstrating. Things change slowly, but things change." I'll go along with that.

The activists in the strike did not come out of nowhere. In Quebec, ever since the alter-globalization surge in the early 2000s, the opposition to right-wing economic and social policies has consolidated. The spring of 2012 should be seen as part of that process: from the Summit of the Americas in 2001, to the founding of Québec solidaire[4] in 2006, from the creation of the Institut de recherche et d'information socio-économique (Institute for socio-economic research and information) in 2001 to the student strike of 2005, and on to the anti–shale gas mobilization in 2010, another Quebec has been on the march for some time now. We are on a long road, and, like some forest roads, it may even turn out to be a dead end. But if we stay on the side of the road, we will surely not get very far.

I spoke with a young militant of the Indigenous movement Idle No More who compared mobilization to a wave. We see and hear it when it hits the shore, and we get the impression that it withdraws as quickly as it came, without leaving a trace. What we often forget, he said, is that it is invariably followed by a new wave, and that it always emerges from the same ocean. What appears to us to be two successive, distinct waves is in fact the result of the same ongoing movement. Slowly but inexorably, the shoreline is transformed. The wave of the *carrés rouges* may appear to have withdrawn swiftly without leaving a trace, but it will return even stronger than before.

Epilogue

We carry within us a fireplace flame, a woodstove fire, to fight against the great darkness of individualist ideas heated with coal. We are a dense grove; a sugary sap runs through our proud body, a body rooted like an oak, the tree that saw Radisson, Donnacona, that saw the man who saw the man who saw the bear. This ain't no story that happened to the friend of a friend of a cousin, it's our story tightly knit with goose wool, a story pointed straight at the shared future, something like the beginning of an end in a land that for a long time just barely made it through, with its heart in its mouth, but that sets out this time with anything but a dustpan demeanour.

— Fermaille Tremblay

We all have our theories about the meaning of the events discussed here, and it seems unlikely that any of us will claim to know the whole story. But we are all talking about the same thing, which in itself is quite something. Much has been said about polarization, but the divisions and confrontations, paradoxically, brought people closer. Like it or not, our disagreements reminded us that we constitute a people, and that some choices can only be made together. The sociologist Gilles Gagné pointed out to me one day that, throughout the history of Quebec, most of the crucial moments of strife were defused from the outside. The student strike of 2012 was among the few political crises that did not lead to a federal or British intervention. The 1970 October Crisis and the 1990 Oka Crisis, the Patriots' War of 1837–38 and the Conscription Crises of 1917 and 1944 – in every case it was the army or the federal government that stepped in for the endgame. In fact, if the Quebec Spring aroused such strong emotions, it was partly because, through it, Quebec proved to be a mature society. In the debate on our collective future, we were perhaps astonished to discover what it means to be a sovereign people.

The defence of education in Quebec is intrinsically a cultural struggle, one of those struggles that always have existential implications for this land. For fifty years, public universities have been among the levers that we have constructed to ensure the enduring vitality of francophone culture in North America. The current transformation of universities, of which tuition increases are a component, shows that these establishments could cease to assume this cultural role within our society. We are presently witnessing the denationalization of public institutions through the imposition of neoliberal policies. In some countries, the United States, for example, such policies leave the common culture more or less intact, but not in Quebec. Since the Quiet Revolution, we can no longer be reassured with pious vows, hoping, as in bygone days, that our faith will protect the French language. Today we know that our destiny and culture do not depend on Providence and do not reside in a crucifix, but are tied to the political and economic institutions of our society. To give these up would be to give up on ourselves, and that is why right-wing policies cannot easily take root along the shores of the St. Lawrence River. It was no accident that the struggles against the appropriation of natural resources and against shale gas development could so readily blend in with the commotion of the student strike. It was no mere coincidence that the poetry of Gaston Miron[1] was read and heard in the streets during the demonstrations. All these things are connected. Whatever those on the more radical fringes of the movement may think, I believe our spring went beyond the traditional clash between left and right. It expressed our adherence to a model of society that underpins our shared identity and through which we hope to survive as a distinct culture. The fear that Trudeau's Charter of Rights will rob us of Christmas or that multiculturalism will force us to play soccer with turbaned teammates – all such foolishness seems, by comparison, to be a very paltry foundation for our common identity.

The PQ, elected in the wake of the student strike, was obviously incapable of seizing the opportunity that was handed to it. Once in power, it quickly put on its old slippers and started to run the province with the shopkeeper mentality that has been its stock-in-trade ever since Lucien Bouchard was its leader. Which only goes to show the extent to which we are locked into the logic of adaptation and docile management. Apparently we no longer have dreams of freedom and justice, just bills and account statements. Our elites, it seems, have developed an obsessive desire to please the US and the major financial institutions rather than to serve the people of Quebec; this can be seen in the way they treat our universities, of course, but even more in the way they treat the territory and the culture. It can be seen in how they mock our intelligence when they wheedle us into voting for them every four years and then expect us to hush up.

Quebec has nothing to gain from humbly adapting to economic globalization. For too long, a concerted effort has been made to foist on us a social model whose disastrous consequences are everywhere to be seen. For too long, we have been asked to believe that independence means joining the circle of countries that passively comply with the dictates of the rating agencies. The sociologist Marcel Rioux reminded us that "sovereignty is indivisible";[2] it can be achieved only when it is at once political, cultural, and economic. Political autonomy, economic democracy, cultural autonomy, free education – this is the legacy of the Quiet Revolution that we must safeguard so that it may be more effectively renewed. Thus, if there is a lesson to be drawn from the spring of 2012, it is this: It is of the utmost urgency to break with the current political elite, which, as Pierre Vadeboncoeur has noted in *Les grands imbéciles*,[3] is busy repackaging the "rejects of yesteryear" to suit the latest styles.

Of all the encounters that I experienced in the course of the strike, there was one that particularly affected me and that aptly illustrates what I am trying to explain. During the May 22 demonstration, a young woman about eighteen years old stepped up to shake my hand. She looked straight at me and said, "Thank you, Gabriel. Thanks to all of you. You've turned my mother into a Québécoise!" I smiled somewhat mechanically, but what she told me quickly captured my attention: "We've been in Quebec for four years, my mother and I, but my mother had never really left her country. She read only Lebanese newspapers and watched nothing but Lebanese stations on TV. In her mind, what happened in Quebec was none of her concern. And, anyways, she understood none of it." Then her eyes lit up as she explained that the student conflict had changed everything. "My sister and I wore the *carrés rouges* and took part in the marches every night, so my mother was forced to take an interest in what was going on." She said that little by little her mother found herself almost obsessively reading and watching whatever was being said about the student strike. Each night she peppered her daughters with questions about the progress of the movement: dates of meetings, decisions made at the CLASSE convention – she wanted to know everything. Then one evening, after a lively discussion, she exclaimed, "But that's not what we want! We in Quebec want accessible education!" The young woman was radiant as she looked me in the eyes: "'We in Quebec'! I'd never heard my mother say anything like that.... The strike made a Québécoise out of her."

In the spring of 2012 we walked tall, against the prevailing wind, and we were heading toward ourselves.

Saint-Antoine-de-Pontbriand, June 2013

Glossary

ADQ. Initialism for Action démocratique Québec (Democratic action Quebec). The ADQ was a right-wing populist political party founded in 1994. It formed the official opposition after the 2007 Quebec general election only to be reduced to seven seats in the election held the next year. It merged with the Coalition Avenir Quebec (CAQ) in 2012. *See also* CAQ

ANEQ/ANEEQ. Acronym for l'Association nationale des étudiantes et étudiants du Québec (National association of Quebec students). ANEQ/ANEEQ was one of the largest and most active student organizations in Quebec from 1975 until 1994, when it was dissolved.

ASSÉ. Acronym for l'Association pour une solidarité syndicale étudiante (Association for student union solidarity). Founded in 2001 in response to a lack of radicalism in other student organizations, the ASSÉ is one of the three major province-wide student organizations in Quebec. Its direct-democracy structure and alignment with the alter-globalization movement distinguish it from other, more moderate student groups. *See* FECQ; FEUQ

Bill 78. Bill 78, often referred to as Law 78 or the special law, was introduced in May 2012 by the Jean Charest government during the Quebec student strike. It provided draconian measures that curbed civil liberties, levied fines on protesters, and attempted to end the strike by restricting the right to dissent and suspending the winter academic term at striking cégeps and universities.

CAQ. Acronym for Coalition Avenir Québec (Coalition for Quebec's future), a right-wing Quebec political party formed by disgruntled members of the Parti Québécois and Action démocratique Québec. The CAQ won 22 seats (out of 125) and over 23 per cent of the popular vote in the April 2014 elections. *See also* ADQ

Carrés rouges. The *carrés rouges*, red squares, are the squares of cloth worn by protesting students and their supporters during the 2012 Quebec student strike. It became the dominant symbol of opposition to the Liberal government's reactionary economic policies. Anti-poverty activists had introduced the symbol in 2004 to express opposition to higher fees for public services in Quebec.

Carré vert. The *carré vert*, green square, was the symbol worn by students supporting the tuition fee hike and opposed to the 2012 Quebec student strike.

CASSÉÉ. Acronym for Coalition de l'Association pour une solidarité syndicale étudiante élargie (Enlarged coalition of the association for student union solidarity). The CASSÉÉ was a temporary united front coalition group created by the ASSÉ for the duration of the 2005 Quebec student strike to accommodate supporters who were not members of the ASSÉ directly. *See also* CLASSE

Cégep. Acronym for Collège d'enseignement général et professionnel (General and Vocational College), a public post-secondary institution unique to Quebec. The first cégeps opened their doors in 1967 as part of Quebec's Quiet Revolution reforms. Quebec students must obtain a cégep diploma in order to be admitted to a university or exercise certain professions in Quebec.

CLASSE. Acronym for the Coalition large de l'Association pour une solidarité syndicale étudiante (Broad-based coalition of the association for student union solidarity). The CLASSE was a temporary united front coalition group created by the ASSÉ for the duration of the 2012 Quebec student strike to accommodate supporters who were not members of the ASSÉ directly. *See also* CASSÉÉ

FECQ. Initialism for the Fédération étudiante collégiale du Québec (the Quebec college students' federation). Founded in 1989 as a splinter group from the ANEQ/ANEEQ, the FECQ is one of the three major province-wide student organizations in Quebec and exclusively represents cégep students (and those from one private college). *See* ASSÉ; FEUQ

FEUQ. Initialism for the Fédération étudiante universitaire du Québec (the Quebec university students' federation). Like its cégep counterpart, the FECQ, the FEUQ was founded in 1989 as a splinter group from the ANEQ/ANEEQ. The FEUQ is one of the three major province-wide student organizations in Quebec and exclusively represents university students. *See* ASSÉ; FECQ

MNA. Initialism for Member of the National Assembly of Quebec. *See also* National Assembly

National Assembly. Officially the National Assembly of Quebec, the National Assembly is the provincial legislature of Quebec. *See also* MNA

OECD. Initialism for the Organisation for Economic Co-operation and Development.

PLQ. Initialism for the Parti libéral du Québec (the Quebec Liberal Party). Historically a centre-left party favouring considerable autonomy for Quebec within the Canadian federation, the party underwent a marked shift to the right as of the 1990s. It currently holds power in the National Assembly, having won a majority (70 seats out of 125, 41.5 per cent of the popular vote) in the April 2014 election.

PQ. Initialism for the Parti Québécois, the principal sovereigntist party in Quebec. Founded in 1968 under the leadership of René Lévesque, the PQ has traditionally been situated to the left of the Liberal Party, but the social-democratic elements of its program have been steadily eroded since the late 1990s. It is presently the official opposition, after winning thirty seats in the April 2014 election and 25.4 per cent of the popular vote.

Québec solidaire (QS). A left-wing political party in Quebec founded in 2006. Québec solidaire's platform identifies it as green, progressive, democratic, feminist, alter-globalizationist, pluralist, and sovereign-tist. It won three seats (7.6 per cent of the popular vote) in the April 2014 provincial election.

SPVM. Initialism for the Service de police de la Ville de Montréal, the City of Montreal's police service.

SQ. Initialism for the Sûreté du Québec, Quebec's provincial police force.

UCL. Initialism for the Union communiste libertaire (Libertarian Communist Union), an anarcho-communist group in Quebec disbanded in March 2014. .

Université du Québec. A province-wide network of universities created in 1968 as part of the Quiet Revolution's major education reforms. It is currently composed of ten component institutions with a total enrolment of about ninety-four thousand.

Glossary for the English edition provided by Lazer Lederhendler.

Notes

Additional notes for the English edition provided by Lazer Lederhendler.

Preface to the English Edition

1 Denis Monière, *Le développement des idéologies au Québec: Des origines à nos jours* (Montreal: Éditions Québec-Amérique, 1977), 320. [This and all other quotations from French-language sources are rendered in our translation, unless otherwise indicated. – Trans.]

Chronology

1 From Maude Bonenfant, Anthony Glinoer, and Martine-Emmanuelle Lapointe, *Le printemps québécois: Une anthologie* (Montreal: Écosociété, 2012). Translated and reprinted by permission of the publisher.

Introduction

1 Clairandrée Cauchy, "Vers de nouvelles hausses de droits de scolarité," *Le Devoir,* June 12, 2009.
2 See Glossary. – Ed.
3 The advisory committee on the economy and public finances, set up and headed by Raymond Bachand as part of the 2010–11 pre-budget consultation process, was composed of four economists whose neoliberal ideological positions were widely known: Pierre Fortin, Robert Gagné, Luc Godbout, and Claude Montmarquette.
4 See Glossary. – Ed.
5 The term *national,* used here to signify "pan-Quebec," derives from the recognition that Quebec constitutes a nation. – Trans.
6 Pierre Bourgault (1934–2003) was a pioneer of the Quebec independentist movement, a cause he defended throughout his multifaceted career as a journalist, politician, university professor, radio host, essayist, and, especially, public speaker. In 1968, as president of the Rassemblement pour l'indépendance nationale (RIN; Alliance for national independence), Bourgault proposed that the RIN be dissolved and that its members join the newly founded Parti Québécois. – Trans.

One: A Twelve-Vote Margin

1 Witness, for instance, the fact that during the 2012 strike the proposed hike was described in the media as an "unfreezing" (*dégel*), an error that was rarely corrected despite student organizations repeatedly pointing out that fees in Quebec had been unfrozen for five years.
2 Plan Nord (Plan for the north) is the Quebec government's comprehensive economic strategy for resource extraction in Quebec's northern regions. It was first introduced in May 2011 by Premier Jean Charest. – Trans.

Two: A Generation No One Was Counting On

1 See Glossary. – Ed.
2 In other words, the Parti Québécois of today has abandoned the social-democratic roots associated with the leadership of René Lévesque from 1968 to 1985 in favour of the neoliberal policies of Lucien Bouchard's leadership from 1996 to 2001. – Trans.

Three: The Hatred of Democracy

1 Richard Martineau, "Quelle démocratie?" *Journal de Montréal*, August 10, 2012.
2 See Glossary. – Ed.
3 The Charbonneau Commission was created by the government of Quebec in November 2011 to conduct a public inquiry into allegedly corrupt practices involving Quebec's construction industry and public officials. The commission is chaired by Justice France Charbonneau. Its final report has not yet been completed as of the time of writing. – Trans.
4 See Glossary under "Bill 78." – Ed.
5 Members or supporters of the political party Coalition Avenir Québec (CAQ) are colloquially referred to as "caquistes," or CAQists. – Trans.
6 Jacques Généreux, *La dissociété* (Paris: Seuil, 2011), 67.
7 André Pratte, "La tyrannie de la minorité," *La Presse*, April 20, 2012.
8 André Pratte, "De la rue au vote," *La Presse*, May 9, 2012.
9 Pratte, "La tyrannie,"
10 The *Journal de Montréal* is a daily tabloid newspaper published in Montreal by Sun Media, a subsidiary of Quebecor Media. With well over three hundred thousand readers, it has the largest circulation of any French-language newspaper in North America. *La Presse*, the *Journal de Montréal*'s main competitor, was founded in 1884 and is owned today by Groupe Gesca, a subsidiary of Power Corporation of Canada. – Trans.
11 Paul Krugman, *The Conscience of a Liberal* (New York: W.W. Norton, 2007), 70. Italics in original.
12 Ibid.

Four: The Revolt of the Rich

1 Valérie Vierstraete, *Les frais de scolarité, l'aide financière et la fréquentation des établissements d'enseignement post-secondaire* (Quebec: Quebec Department of Education, Recreation, and Sports, 2007).

2 At the time of the 2012 Quebec student strike, Julie Boulet served as Quebec's minister of employment and social solidarity, Pierre Moreau as its minister of transport, and Jean-Marc Fournier as its minister of justice. – Trans.

3 Guy Rocher is a noted Quebec sociologist and academic who, as co-author of the 1961–66 Parent Commission's final report, helped to overhaul the province's education system. Jean Garon (1938–2014) was a founding member of the Parti Québécois and held the agriculture portfolio and, later, the education portfolio in various PQ cabinets. Jean Cournoyer is a television and radio host and a former Liberal politician who served in the Bourassa cabinet as minister of labour during the turbulent period of 1970–75. Jacques Parizeau is an economist and has been a key actor in the Quebec independentist movement since the late 1960s; he was leader of the Parti Québécois from 1988 to 1996 and, as premier of Quebec from 1994 to 1996, played a central role in the 1995 referendum. Lise Payette is a feminist, journalist, author, and former politician who served in René Lévesque's cabinet as Quebec's status of women minister from 1979 to 1981. Jacques-Yvan Morin is a former law professor and Parti Québécois politician who held several important ministerial portfolios under the premiership of René Lévesque. – Trans.

4 Lisa-Marie Gervais, "Aux recteurs de faire des efforts, dit Jean Garon," *Le Devoir*, April 17, 2012.

5 Alexandre Shields, "Universités – La gratuité est réaliste, dit Jacques Parizeau," *Le Devoir*, February 12, 2013.

6 Guy Rocher, "Une mentalité commerciale," in Éric Martin and Maxime Ouellet, *Université inc.* (Montreal: Lux, 2011), 125.

7 Lise Payette, "Les jeunes payent le prix, et c'est toute notre société qui s'appauvrit," in Martin and Ouellet, *Université inc.*, 129.

8 The final report of the Parent Commission, officially the *Quebec Royal Commission of Inquiry on Education*, was presided over by the vice-rector of Laval University, Mgr. Alphonse-Marie Parent. It called for major education reforms in Quebec, leading to, among other results, the end of the Church's control over schools, the creation of a Quebec Ministry of Education, the cégep system, and greater access to higher education. Published in 1963–64, the report was a crucial element of the Quiet Revolution. – Trans.

9 Simon Langlois, "Mutation des classes moyennes au Québec entre 1982 et 2008," *Le cahiers des Dix*, no. 64 (2010): 130.

10 Stéphane Crespo, *L'inégalité de revenus au Québec 1979–2004. Les contributions de composantes de revenu selon le cycle économique* (Quebec: Institut de la statistique du Québec, 2007), 64.

11 Langlois, "Mutations des classes moyennes," 136.

12 Gervais, "Aux recteurs de faire des efforts."

13 Jean-François Lisée was elected to the National Assembly in 2012 under the Parti Québécois banner and was a minister in Pauline Marois's short-lived government (2012–14). Previously, he was well known as a political analyst, journalist, author,

and sovereigntist theoritician, and he was an advisor to Jacques Parizeau and Lucien Bouchard. As of this writing, he is a contender in the forthcoming PQ leadership race. – Trans.

14 CHOI-FM, better known locally as Radio X, is a controversial right-wing radio station in Quebec City. Its popularity soared in the early 2000s thanks to the "trash radio" style of its morning man, Jeff Fillion, who was dismissed in 2005 in the wake of a costly libel suit against the station. – Trans.

15 Paul Krugman, "The Tax-Cut Con," *New York Times*, September 14, 2003, www .nytimes.com.

16 Simon Tremblay-Pepin, "Les médias et la hausse des frais de scolarité de 2005 à 2010 – 1ère partie," *Institut de recherche et d'informations socio-économique (IRIS)*, February 4, 2013, http://iris-recherche.qc.ca.

17 Guy Breton has been the rector of the Université de Montréal since 2010. – Trans.

18 Martine Letarte, "Université de Montréal – Une troisième avenue pour les partenariats," *Le Devoir*, January 28, 2012.

19 Hannah Arendt, *The Human Condition* (Chicago: University of Chicago Press, 1998 [1958]), location 4901. Kindle edition.

20 Mauricio Lazzarato, *La fabrique de l'homme endetté, essai sur la condition néolibérale* (Paris: Éditions Amsterdam, 2011), 81.

21 Robert Sibley, "Chomsky talks fear in western society: Activist makes his case to Carleton audience," *Ottawa Citizen*, April 9, 2011, D3.

22 Ibid.

23 Figures are as of the time of writing. – Ed.

24 In *Université inc.*, Éric Martin and Maxime Ouellet, referring to the work of the Institut de recherche et d'informations socio-économiques, note that similar results were observed in Quebec during the 1990s, when, in the wake of a significant rise in tuition, the level of enrolment decreased by over 5 per cent between 1992–93 and 1997–98, while it increased markedly during the periods of frozen fees before and after the rise.

Five: Excellence?

1 Joseph Facal, former PQ minister and head of Quebec's Treasury Board; Lucien Bouchard, former PQ leader and premier of Quebec; Michel Audet, former Liberal cabinet member, notably as minister of finance; Monique Jérôme-Forget, former Liberal cabinet member, notably as minister of finance and head of the Treasury Board; Claude Montmarquette, professor of economics at the Université de Montréal; Yves-Thomas Dorval, head of the Quebec Employers Council; Robert Lacroix, former rector of the Université de Montréal. This group is closely associated with neoliberalism in Quebec, more specifically with the controversial neoliberal manifesto "Pour un Québec lucide" ("For a clear-sighted Quebec"), published in 2005 and signed by twelve personalities, including Bouchard, Facal, Montmarquette, and Lacroix. – Trans.

2 Joseph Facal et al., "Universités – Faisons le choix de l'excellence," *Le Devoir*, May 2, 2012.

3 Bill Readings, *Dans les ruines de l'université* (Montreal: Lux, 2013).

4 Jacques Derrida, "The future of the profession or the university without condition (thanks to the 'Humanities,' what *could take place* tomorrow)," in Tom Cohen, ed.,

Jacques Derrida and the Humanities: A Critical Reader (Cambridge, UK: Cambridge University Press, 2002), 25. Italics in original.

5 Judith Woodsworth left her position as rector amid controversy in December 2010. She received a generous separation allowance of $700,000; it is not clear whether she resigned or was dismissed. As rector, she had attended the Vancouver Olympic Games at the expense of Bell Canada. A few months later, Concordia awarded Bell a contract worth $900,000. The university has always denied any conflict of interest. See Kathleen Lévesque, "Concordia tente de calmer le jeu," *Le Devoir*, January 11, 2011. The excerpt from Ms. Woodsworth's address is in our translation.

6 Martin and Ouellet, *Université inc.* Italics in original.

7 The *Journal de Québec* is a daily tabloid newspaper published in Quebec City. Like the *Journal de Montréal*, it is owned by Quebecor's media subsidary Sun Media. – Trans.

8 Daphnée Dion-Viens, "Augmentation du salaire du recteur de l'Université Laval: décision mal avisée," *Le Soleil*, March 12, 2011.

9 Desjardins was president of the FEUQ during the strike. – Trans.

10 Quoted in Martin and Ouellet, *Université inc.*, 109.

11 Christian Laval, *L'école n'est pas une entreprise* (Paris: La Découverte, 2004), 22. Italics in original.

12 Former PQ minister of finance and co-founder and leader of the Coalition Avenir Québec. – Trans.

13 Marie-Andrée Chouinard, "Financement de l'enseignement supérieur – La question de 3 milliards," *Le Devoir*, January 12, 2013.

14 Chris Hedges, *Empire of Illusion: The End of Literacy and the Triumph of Spectacle* (Toronto: Vintage, 2010).

15 Laval, *L'école n'est pas une entreprise*, 56.

16 Ibid.

17 Ibid.

18 Howard Hotson, "Don't Look to the Ivy League," *London Review of Books* 33, no. 10 (May 19, 2011): 20–22.

19 "Nope, Just Debt," *The Economist*, October 29, 2011, www.economist.com.

20 Throughout the student strike, mass demonstrations were regularly held on the twenty-second day of each month. – Trans.

21 Sheryl Nance-Nash, "Student Loan Debt: $1 Trillion and Counting," *Forbes*, March 22, 2012, www.forbes.com.

22 Quoted in Martin and Ouellet, *Université inc.*

23 Mathieu Bock-Côté is a pro-independence sociologist, essayist, and columnist known for his deeply conservative brand of Quebec nationalism. – Trans.

24 Marcel Rioux, "Politique et culture," in *La culture comme refus de l'économisme: Écrits de Marcel Rioux*, eds. Jacques Hamel, Julien Forgues Lecavalier, and Marcel Fournier (Montreal: Presses de l'Université de Montréal, 2010).

25 The *cours classiques* refers to Quebec's traditional eight-year, humanities-oriented curriculum that prepared students (mostly from affluent families) for university before the major reforms of the Quiet Revolution, especially the creation of the cégep system. – Trans.

26 See Glossary. – Ed.

Six: Soldiers without a Commander?

1 Simon Durivage is a popular host on the Radio-Canada news program *RDI en Direct* (*RDILive*) on the CBC's French-language, twenty-four-hour news channel Réseau de l'information (RDI). – Trans.

2 Jeanne Reynolds and Gabriel Nadeau-Dubois acted as CLASSE co-spokespersons during the Quebec student strike. – Trans.

3 See Glossary. – Ed.

4 Nathalie Collard, "Conflit étudiant dans les médias: trop d'opinions, pas assez d'analyses," *La Presse*, June 10, 2012.

5 Chantal Francoeur, *Informer ou in-former: le formats journalistiques au service du statu quo* (Montreal: Université du Québec à Montréal, 2012), 21.

6 Ibid., 22.

7 President of the FECQ. – Trans.

8 Liza Frulla, a well-known media personality, is a former Liberal politician: Quebec MNA 1989–1998, MP 2002–2006, and member of the Cabinet of Prime Minister Paul Martin. – Trans.

9 In Quebec, ever since the adoption of the *Act respecting the accreditation and financing of students' associations*, student organizations in the cégeps and universities hold a monopoly on student representation. Hence, as would be the case with a labour union, students are automatically members of their association, to which they pay dues by default. They can, of course, withdraw from the association, but it is up to them to take the necessary steps.

10 For an in-depth analysis of the part played by social media during the 2012 student strike, see (my former colleagues) Renaud Poirier-St-Pierre and Philippe Éthier, *De l'école à la rue: Dans les coulisses d'une grève étudiante* (Montreal: Éditions Écosociété, 2013).

11 The Salon Plan Nord was a meeting of hundreds of politicians, investors, and business leaders in Montreal to discuss the government's plans for resource extraction in northern Quebec at the Montreal Palais des congrès (Convention Centre). – Trans.

Seven: Collective Hysteria

1 The Montreal subway.

2 Dominic Maurais, "Les Soviets de salon," *Le Journal de Québec*, April 21, 2012.

3 "Voice of Facts," a pun on *voie de fait*, meaning "assault." – Trans.

4 Maurais, "Les Soviets."

5 Quebecor, one of Canada's largest media corporations, is the owner of the *Journal de Québec*, as well as several other French- and English-language broadcasting groups and tabloid newspapers. – Trans.

6 The decision can be consulted online at http://conseildepresse.qc.ca/decisions/d2012-04-091.

7 Centre d'études sur les médias, *La presse quotidienne* (Quebec: Université Laval, 2011), www.cem.ulaval.ca.

8 These expressions were used respectively by Richard Martineau, "Six mois plus tard," *Le Journal de Montréal*, December 22, 2012, and "L'âge des extrêmes," *Le Journal de Montréal*, June 2, 2012; Benoît Aubin, "Érosion démocratique," *Le Jour-*

nal de Montréal, May 19, 2012, and "La loi, l'ordre et le bon gouvernement," *Le Journal de Montréal*, May 10, 2012; Martineau, "Les brutes," *Le Journal de Montréal*, May 5, 2012; and Éric Duhaime, "Balade antiterroriste dans le métro," *Le Journal de Québec*, May 13, 2012.

9   These expressions were used respectively by Aubin, "La loi, l'ordre, et le bon gouvernement"; Mathieu Bock-Côté, "Un extrémisme destructeur," *Le Journal de Montréal*, May 10, 2012; and Martineau, "Six mois plus tard."

10 Nathalie Elgraby, "Résister au chaos," *Le Journal de Montréal*, May 17, 2012.

11 Claude Giguère, "Gendron traite les profs de crasseux," *Montréal Express*, August 7, 2012.

12 These terms were used respectively by Alain Dubuc, "Un braquage surréaliste," *La Presse*, May 2, 2012, and Aubin, "La loi, l'ordre, et le bon gouvernement."

13 Bock-Côté, "Un extrémisme destructeur."

14 Alain Dubuc, "Chercher l'erreur," *La Presse*, May 28, 2012.

15 Mercier is a provincial electoral district in Montreal that since 2008 has been represented in the National Assembly by Amir Khadir of the left-wing party Québec solidaire. – Trans.

16 Joseph Facal, *Le Journal de Montréal*, June 11, 2012. In this column, Mr. Facal related his dream of a Quebec fallen under the yoke of the left. Strangely, the acronym of this tyrannical regime is the same, in French, as that of the Unité permanente anticorruption (Permanent anti-corruption unit) – the UPAC – of the Sûreté du Québec (SQ), the Quebec provincial police. Was this intentional or a mere slip of the pen? Either way, it would appear that in Joseph Facal's subconscious the fight against corruption and the fight against capitalism target the same people, with whom he seems to identify.

17 Benoît Aubin, "La gauche égoïste," *Le Journal de Montréal*, June 4, 2012.

18 André Pratte, "Les complices," *La Presse*, April 17, 2012.

19 Alain Dubuc, "La grave erreur de Madame Marois," *La Presse*, June 4, 2012.

20 Aubin, "La gauche égoïste."

21 Benoît Aubin, "Un détournement de débat politique," *Le Journal de Montréal*, May 24, 2012.

22 Isabelle Maréchal, "Le carré de la honte," *Le Journal de Montréal*, May 20, 2012.

23 Christian Dufour, "Le droit d'abuser," *Le Journal de Montréal*, May 29, 2012.

24 Gilbert Lavoie, "Le syndrome des casseroles," *Le Soleil*, June 2, 2012.

25 Duhaime, "Balade antiterroriste dans le métro."

26 Aubin, "Un détournement de débat politique."

27 Richard Martineau, "Ce que la crise m'a appris," *Le Journal de Montréal*, June 25, 2012.

28 The reference, of course, is to Bush's address to Congress on September 20, 2001, shortly after the September 11 attacks, when he famously declared, "Either you are with us or you are with the terrorists."

29 André Pratte, "Retour au calme: un devoir national," *La Presse*, May 22, 2012.

30 André Pratte, "Le bâton et le serpent," *La Presse*, May 19, 2012.

31 "Claude Poirier – 'Fuck Y'all' Les Étudiants et Étudiantes." YouTube video, 3:17, posted by "Pathetik Degenerate," May 15, 2012, www.youtube.com.

32 Alain Dubuc, "L'erreur libérale," *La Presse*, May 4, 2012.

Eight: At the Parthenais Detention Centre

1 The Parthenais Detention Centre is a prison that spans three floors of the SQ headquarters in Montreal. It is known in particular for its use during the October Crisis as a long-term holding centre for political prisoners and suspected FLQ members and sympathizers in harsh conditions, resulting in hunger strikes, riots, and public pressure to close the facility. – Trans.

2 Robert Dutil, minister of public security. – Trans.

3 Antoine Robitaille, "Crise étudiante: l'horizon est bouché," *Le Devoir*, April 27, 2012.

4 Ligue des droits et libertés, Association des juristes progressistes, and Comité légal de la classe, *Répression, discrimination et grève étudiante: analyse et témoignages*, April 2013, http://ajpquebec.org.

5 Ibid., 6.

6 Philippe Tesceira-Lessard, "Un manifestant blessé envisage de porter plainte," *La Presse*, May 3, 2012.

7 Ligue des droits et libertés et al., *Répression, discrimination et grève étudiante*, 33.

8 Michèle Ouimet, "Bourrés de préjugés, les policiers?" *La Presse*, May 30, 2012.

9 A Commission spéciale d'examen des événements du printemps 2012 (Special commission to examine the events of the spring of 2012), commonly known as the Commission Ménard (after its chairman, Serge Ménard), was created by the PQ government on May 8, 2013. The Commission's report was submitted in March 2014. The commission had no powers of investigation or interrogation. Participation was voluntary, and the police refused to take part. As a result, no further light has actually been shed on the police's actions in 2012. – Trans.

Nine: In Defiance

1 The Salon bleu, the Blue hall, is where the deliberations of the National Assembly of Quebec take place. It is located in the Hôtel du Parlement (Parliament Building) in Quebec City. – Trans.

2 The October Crisis of 1970 refers to a series of events that started with the kidnapping of the British trade commissioner James Cross by a cell of the Front de Libération du Québec (FLQ, Quebec liberation front). In accordance with one of the FLQ's demands, its manifesto was broadcast by a Montreal radio station on October 7, and the next day on Radio-Canada's television network. Two days later, Quebec's labour minister, Pierre Laporte, was kidnapped by another FLQ cell. On October 15, a large pro-FLQ rally was held in a Montreal arena; Canadian prime minister Pierre Trudeau invoked the *War Measures Act*, deploying army troops in Montreal and other major cities. A day later, the Sûreté du Québec arrested 457 people suspected of ties or sympathies with the FLQ or other far-left groups. James Cross would be released on December 4 in exchange for safe conduct to Cuba for his kidnappers. Pierre Laporte was found dead on October 17. His kidnappers (except for one apprehended on November 5) were arrested on December 28, 1970, marking the official end of the crisis; they would eventually be sentenced to long prison terms for their various roles in the events leading to Laporte's death. – Trans.

3 Sophie-Hélène Lebeuf, "Le ministre Bachand préfère les casseroles aux casseurs," Radio-Canada, May 25, 2012, www.radio-canada.ca.

4 Tommy Chouinard, "Manifestations: 'assez c'est assez!' tonne Raymond Bachand," *La Presse*, May 15, 2012.

5 Tommy Chouinard, "Désobéissance civile: Jean-Marc Fournier condamne le choix de la CLASSE," *La Presse*, May 22, 2012.

6 Denise Bombardier, "La rue a gagné," *Le Devoir*, May 26, 2012.

7 Pierre Vadeboncoeur (1920–2010) was an influential trade unionist and essayist. – Trans.

8 Émilie-Gamelin square is a small downtown park near the main campus of the Université du Québec à Montréal. It often serves as a gathering place for political rallies and marches. – Trans.

9 Arrested in October 1970 under the *War Measures Act*, Michel Chartrand, Pierre Vallières, Charles Gagnon, Robert Lemieux, and Jacques Larue-Langlois were charged with "seditious conspiracy." On the very first day of the spectacular *procès des Cinq*, January 8, 1971, Michel Chartrand was convicted four times for contempt of court. All the accused would later be acquitted.

Ten: Under the Shield of the Law

1 "Université Laval: un autre étudiant réclame une injonction pour retourner en classe," Radio-Canada, April 12, 2012, www.radio-canada.ca.

2 Quoted in Michel Corbeil, "Laurent Proulx, le champion du libre accès," *Le Soleil*, April 7, 2012, www.lapresse.ca.

3 Lessard c. Cégep de Sherbrooke, [2012] QCCS 1669. The decision is available online at www.jugements.qc.ca.

4 Quoted in Antoine Robitaille, "Des idées en l'ère – Jean Charest, chef gréviste," *Le Devoir*, May 19, 2012.

5 "Hausse des frais de scolarité; les grèves étudiantes déclenchées," *TVA Nouvelles*, February 14, 2012, http://tvanouvelles.ca. Italics added.

6 Christian Brunelle, "Injonctions et grève étudiante – La primauté de droit en péril," *Le Devoir*, April 30, 2012.

7 Morasse c. Nadeau-Dubois, [2012] QCCS 5438. The decision is available online at http://jugements.qc.ca.

8 Yves Boisvert, "La culpabilité douteuse de GND," *La Presse*, November 8, 2012.

9 Michel Chartrand et al., *Le procès des Cinq* (Montreal: Lux, 2010), 96.

10 Decision quoted by Yves Boisvert, "La solution n'est pas judiciaire," *La Presse*, May 5, 2012, www.lapresse.ca.

11 Morasse c. Nadeau-Dubois.

12 Morasse c. Nadeau-Dubois, [2012] QCCS 6101. The decision is available online at www.jugements.qc.ca.

13 "Ouverture des tribunaux Montréal. Allocution prononcée par l'honorable François Rolland, juge en chef," Superior Court of Quebec, September 6, 2012, www.barreaudemontreal.qc.ca. Note: This document is no longer available online. The following page references are to the author's copy of the PDF. – Trans.

14 Ibid., 3.

15 Ibid., 6.
16 Ibid., 8.
17 Ibid., 9.
18 Ibid., 10.
19 Ibid., 9.

Eleven: All for What?

1 Members of the Parti Québecois (PQ), an acronym of the party's initials. – Trans.
2 In 1972 the province's three largest union federations formed a united front against the government during the public sector contract negotiations. The key demand was simple and forceful, somewhat like that of the spring of 2012: a minimum weekly wage of $100. The idea, conceived by the president of the Confédération des syndicats nationaux (Confederation of National Trade Unions), Marcel Pépin, was at first thought unrealistic, but the strikers eventually rallied behind it. It was a gruelling conflict that culminated in the adoption of a special law. Having called for the strike to continue regardless, the three union leaders were jailed. Throughout Quebec, the response was a wave of broad-based demonstrations that often turned into riots.
3 Gilles Vigneault is a popular Québécois poet, singer-songwriter, and long-standing supporter of the independentist cause. – Trans.
4 See Glossary. – Ed.

Epilogue

1 Gaston Miron (1928–1996) was a major poet and writer of the Quiet Revolution and an outspoken advocate of independence for Quebec. – Trans.
2 Marcel Rioux, "Politique et culture."
3 Pierre Vadeboncoeur, *Les grands imbéciles* (Montreal: Lux, 2008).

Index